Just Like Us

Round the Cradle, the Cross and the Crown

David Gurney

authorHOUSE®

AuthorHouse™ UK Ltd.
500 Avebury Boulevard
Central Milton Keynes, MK9 2BE
www.authorhouse.co.uk
Phone: 08001974150

Published by AuthorHouse 8/29/12

ISBN: 978-1-4772-2293-5 (sc)
ISBN: 978-1-4772-2292-8 (hc)
ISBN: 978-1-4772-2294-2 (e)

For our grandchildren
and godchildren,
great-nephews,
and great-nieces

Contents

Just like Us
I. Round the Cradle

ELIZABETH

I suppose I'm what you would call a real countrywoman. I've always lived in this village, and the older I get, the more I love it. Life here in the hills is so tranquil and unhurried. Where in the city could you get such a sweeping view as I can enjoy sitting right here at my own front door? From what my husband Zacharias tells me about Jerusalem, I count myself favoured indeed with our lovely little home here in the serenity and safety of the hills. He has to go to Jerusalem regularly because he's a priest, and his name is on the Temple duty roster. Of course, I've been there with him many a time in my younger days, but now that I'm older, I find travel difficult and tiring, so I'm content to stay at home and wait eagerly to hear all he has to tell me when he gets back.

In all the years we've been married, he's never had anything to tell me to compare with what he said when he came home last time – or rather, with what he didn't say. I had a bad shock when he made no answer to my welcome as he stooped to enter our house through that little door there.

"Whatever's the matter with you, Zachary?" I cried out. He rummaged through his travelling bag and pulled out his writing things.

1

I watched in growing dismay as he wrote "I cannot speak". By the end of the day he'd written down the whole story for me. Apparently he'd filled the censer with incense on the last day of his duty, ignited it, and was swinging it in front of the altar when he became aware of a figure standing there, half-hidden by the sweet-smelling smoke billowing from the censer.

The shock nearly made him drop it, but the messenger's first words were, "Do not be afraid, Zacharias; your prayer has been heard. Your wife Elizabeth will bear you a son, and you are to give him the name John", and he went on to make a marvellous prophecy about the promised boy.

Now the one great grief of our long and happy marriage has been that we never had a family. We have prayed and prayed for a child, and when I've been on my own, I've wept and wept for want of one, but it's many years now that my periods stopped. I long ago came to accept that childlessness was God's will for me. But dear Zacharias has gone on all this time persisting in prayer for a baby. When he was given a direct answer to his prayer, would you believe, he just couldn't accept it? From what he wrote down for me, I gather he more or less demanded some sort of sign – from God's own messenger, mind you – that what he'd promised would actually happen! I can't tell you how terrified I was when I read all this. The angel drew himself up to his full height and delivered the stinging rebuke that he was Gabriel, who stands in the presence of God himself, and that because my husband had not believed his words, he would not be able to speak until the day they came true.

Now, although my family is directly descended from Moses's brother Aaron, and although my husband is a priest, I'm a perfectly ordinary Jewess, with no pretensions to deep knowledge of the Law or of the finer points of theological controversy. I have tried all my life to live pleasing to God by keeping the commandments and by observing all the religious rituals required by our rulers and rabbis. As a result, I'm blessed with a quietly confident faith. I just knew, don't ask me how, that God would honour His promise. So it was no surprise to me when I became aware that, at long last, after so many years of hope and disappointment, I was pregnant.

Nothing in this life is perfect, of course. I've already said how content I am with life in my native village here in the hill country; but inevitably, the smaller the community, the less chance there is of keeping a secret. All the same, I managed to conceal my condition for fully five months. I went out as little as possible, tried to avoid speaking to anyone unnecessarily, and of course, breathed not a word to any relatives, friends, or visitors. I naturally wanted to be absolutely certain that I was carrying before I broke the news. In any case, anything can happen, especially in the early days, can't it? But when I was six months gone, I had a completely unexpected but hugely delightful experience.

I was resting quietly one day when there was a knock at the door. Zacharias answered it, and to my utter amazement, in came a young woman who, although I had not seen her before, I instantly realised was Mary, a distant relative of mine who lives in Nazareth in Galilee, some sixty miles or more to the north of us.

"Whatever brings you here?" I cried. "Is it good news or bad?" I need hardly have asked; she had an air of calmness about her which said more than any words could that she was at peace, both outwardly with the world and inwardly with herself.

"Elizabeth, my dear," she said, in a low, gentle voice, "I heard your wonderful news, and I simply had to come and share your joy."

I was completely taken aback. After all my efforts to keep my secret, it appeared that Mary, living at the other end of the country, knew all about it. Naturally, I asked her how she had heard that I was going to have a baby.

"Wait till I've seen to the donkey," she said, with a winning smile, but Zacharias had already led him round to the back of the house and was giving him feed and water. So Mary settled herself down, and what she told us that afternoon dramatically confirmed our growing realisation that now, almost at the end of our lives, God was at last intervening to fulfil his age-long promises by sending the Messiah to save us from our enemies.

Mary said she'd been getting on with her housework one day when she became aware that there was another person in the room. She spun round and was terrified to see a young man dressed all in white standing there; but he gave her a most respectful greeting, describing her as highly favoured and assuring her that the Lord was with her. I simply had to interrupt to say that that was exactly what happened to Zacharias in the Temple at Jerusalem. But the similarity didn't stop there. Just as Gabriel had promised us our baby, so he went on to tell Mary that she was going to become a mother, but whereas Zacharias and I were overjoyed at our news, Mary was at first very upset by hers. You see, she's engaged to a very nice chap in Nazareth, a carpenter by

3

trade, quite a bit older than she is but by all accounts a very steady, law-abiding fellow. They hadn't planned to marry for quite a few months yet, maybe even a year or more. Mary said as much to the angel, but the things he said about the boy she would bear were so astonishing that, as she said to us both, she realised that whatever other people might say about her, she had actually been chosen by God for the overwhelming privilege of being the mother of the Messiah. Gabriel told Mary that her son was to be named Jesus, which, as you know, means *God is our salvation*, but the angel also said that he would be called *Son of the Most High*, or even *Son of God*, and that God would give him the throne of his ancestor King David, and he would reign for ever.

Now how would you react to talk like that? Well, it all depends on who's doing the talking, doesn't it? As I said, I had not met Mary before, but of course I'd heard about her. Relatives had said she was very devout, but I could tell straightaway that there was a very great deal more to her than the standard regular ritual observances of the majority of folks. She radiated quiet trust, deep peace, and genuine submission to God, which were all wholly unaffected. Her eyes, her posture, her words, the tone of her voice, her attitude – all unconsciously indicated a depth of sincerity and understanding which rendered me as dumb for the rest of that day as Zacharias had been for the last six months. We both realised that we were in the presence of someone whose relationship with God and acceptance of his will were so much more profound and challenging than anything that either of us had ever experienced or even aspired to.

Mary stayed with us for three months before she returned to Nazareth. The night before she left, she sang to us a song of praise she had composed. It was quite simply the most beautiful thing I have ever heard; it really inspired dear Zacharias, who promptly produced his own hymn when our baby was born. Of course, the neighbours all assumed that he would be called Zacharias, after his father, but I insisted that he was to be called John. No sooner had Zacharias written 'His name is John', than he got his speech back – exactly as he had been promised.

We partied for days; the whole village joined in, and I declare I haven't got over the exhaustion yet. But my beautiful baby boy loved every minute of it – and he's gone from strength to strength ever since.

JOSEPH

It is not easy being a known descendent of a deposed royal family. True, it has been several centuries since the last of my ancestors actually sat on the throne of Judah, but all my life I have had to be aware of potential danger, for we are an occupied people, and inevitably the occupying power is suspicious of contemporary representatives of legitimate authority. Because of my well-documented direct descent from King David, it is certain that I have always been seen as a possible centre around which disaffected nationalist elements might try to concentrate their opposition to the Roman regime. I have tried not to become paranoid about all this, but the simple fact is that I am actually in danger on two fronts. The greater danger threatens from the reigning Idumaean dynasty. They owe their position solely to the Roman power and know that they could lose it considerably more easily than they gained it. They feel particularly vulnerable because they are not true-born Jews and are therefore suspect in the eyes of the people who are supposed to be subject to them.

So the basic instinct for self-preservation has dictated that I live very circumspectly. I have thought it wise to settle in Galilee, well away from the centre of political life in Jerusalem and Judaea. I have been fortunate in being able to make a reasonable living out of the carpenter's trade that I was taught when I was a boy.

But the circumstances of my life which I have just briefly outlined have resulted in my becoming what some have described as a very private man. I acknowledge that the description is just. I tend to keep myself to myself, and I am wary of committing myself too deeply to anyone else – or at least I was until I met Mary. I realise that I tend to look inwards for reassurance rather than outwards to external authority. This tendency was dramatically reinforced when Mary said that she was pregnant.

I cannot begin to convey the devastating effect her simple words had on me. I have waited long for marriage; indeed, I have increasingly wondered whether it was ever to be. I had become aware of Mary as she grew up in Nazareth, and when she was of age, I negotiated with her parents for a contract of betrothal – my own father being by then long since dead. The feeling between us, however, could not have been further from the cold formality suggested by a legal document. Mary was not merely young and beautiful – she is that, but then so are many others. There is an air of calm and peace about her that marks her off from every other girl I have ever met. Her very entry into a room brings with it a balm and benediction of which, I am convinced, she is wholly unaware.

But she is very much more than a merely passive paragon of perfection. I have slowly discovered that she is endowed with spiritual perceptions which put her head and shoulders above any religious teachers I have ever met or heard of. I love her deeply, but I have come to mix with that love a profound respect for a person whose very close walk with God sets her apart from the great majority of ordinary people. There is about her an unconscious aura of saintliness that compels a feeling of wondering awe.

The extent to which I have thus unburdened myself is a measure of the shock I experienced when she told me she was expecting a child. Initial disbelief gave way to blank incomprehension, followed by utter perplexity when she gently unfolded to me the favour God had granted her of a visit from the archangel Gabriel. My first reaction was to forbid her any further communication with me. That meant I had to grapple on my own with all the problems raised by her revelation. I spent days agonising over what my reaction should be, but it soon became clear that there were in fact only two possible courses of action. One was to make a formal repudiation of the betrothal contract; that would have amounted to an odious assertion of self-righteousness on my part, which was entirely repugnant to me. I therefore decided to continue with my initial resolve – to break the relationship completely but to do so entirely privately, with no public announcement.

Only a man who has been in a similar situation can understand the torment I suffered in the ensuing weeks. My internal life was thrown into chaos as feelings of anger, betrayal, resentment, and even hatred and thoughts of revenge surged through me, not merely in bewildering succession but in a simultaneous storm of emotional impulses which frightened me by their irrational intensity. It all came to a head one evening when, without any warning, the tension which had built up within me snapped. I burst into floods of tears – I, a full-grown, mature, privately self-disciplined and publicly well-regarded man. I shook with uncontrollable sobbing until eventually, utterly drained, I collapsed onto my bed and fell immediately into a sleep of total exhaustion.

When I eventually awoke, the day was already bright outside. But my first realisation was of complete inner calm and peace. I felt purged of everything evil and defiling, as clean and fresh as the Galilaean countryside on a spring morning of cloudless sunshine after a storm-lashed night of howling wind and driving rain. But then I remembered why I felt so released and renewed. I was able to recall my dream of that night with a completeness and a clarity which gave it more the quality of a vision than of a mere natural dream. A messenger, whom I instinctively knew to be from God, totally restored my faith in Mary by leading me to the realisation that she was to be the mother of the Messiah. Her child was a gift from God, direct to her without any human intervention. But both she and the baby, like any other mother and child, would need the full support of a husband and father – and I was the one, out of all the men in the world, who had been chosen for this awesome honour.

The renewal of our relationship was a rare and precious experience, which must remain private to us alone, but events soon began to develop an accelerating momentum. Official notices appeared in the village, announcing that the Roman emperor had decreed that a census of the population was to be taken and everyone was to return to his or her place of birth for the purpose of the count. It could not have come at a worse time for us. Mary had by now gone full term, and the baby could arrive any day, but I decided to take the personal risk of going to my family town of Bethlehem in Judaea, rather than run the public risk of drawing unfavourable attention to myself by not registering at the required time and place. We were fortunate in having a donkey, so Mary was able to ride, but because I had to walk, it took us three days to cover the sixty or so miles between Nazareth and Bethlehem. Even so, we only just made it – Mary was in labour by the time we arrived.

It was evening when we finally entered the town. The influx of so many people who, like ourselves, had come for the census, meant that there was not a room to be had anywhere, for love or money. In the end, in response to my desperate pleading, a sympathetic innkeeper offered us the stable behind his premises for the night. At just about midnight, with no help from midwife or nurse, Mary gave birth to the boy whom the angel had told both of us separately was to be named Jesus. In the goodness of God, the birth was uncomplicated, and Mary was soon cradling a tiny perfectly formed little one in her smooth young arms, her own appealing loveliness now enhanced by that special radiance which shines in every newly delivered first-time mother.

Inevitably, I suppose, word got round of what was happening in the stable. What with our own elation and the seemingly unending succession of complete strangers looking in to see the baby and wish us well, neither of us got any sleep that night. But quite a while later we had a visit of an altogether different kind, which I admit considerably alarmed me at first. The day after the census was over, I was able to rent a little house, so we stayed on in Bethlehem. Initially, of course, this was to enable Mary to recover, but because it was so near to Jerusalem, we were able to take the baby to the Temple for his presentation ceremony and Mary's purification.

One day, some good while after that, there was a mighty commotion outside our little house. A whole string of camels was blocking the narrow street, and to our speechless astonishment, three very grand-looking foreigners dismounted. Then, stooping to enter our low door, they knelt to lay immensely expensive gifts on the floor at Mary's feet as she sat with the baby on her lap. They did not stay long and departed as majestically as they had arrived; but their visit triggered for me a second vivid night vision. It was made very clear to me that this ostentatious international acknowledgement of the significance of our baby boy would inevitably arouse the murderous vengeance of the usurping King Herod, only three miles away in Jerusalem. Upon realizing this, I woke Mary immediately, and we left Bethlehem there and then, in the dead of night, taking the splendid presents with us but otherwise little more than the clothes we were standing up in.

We travelled south-west as fast as the donkey allowed us to; but my fears were not really laid to rest until we crossed the border into the safety of Egypt.

We have been here some time now, and Mary and I both wonder wistfully whether we shall ever see Jerusalem, Bethlehem, or Nazareth, again. Jesus is growing fast. He's a fine little chap already, and as soon as his hands can grasp timber and tool, I'll start teaching him how to be a carpenter.

THE INNKEEPER

Honestly, sometimes I'm tempted just to pack it all in, go off into the desert on my own, and become a hermit or something. If ever I could find thirty uninterrupted seconds to myself, I reckon I'd sit down and start to take the idea seriously – provided I didn't fall down first, that is, out of sheer exhaustion. Talk about keeping a dog and barking yourself: taking on extra staff just doesn't seem to make the slightest difference whatsoever. I have to gallop around twice as fast merely to keep standing still. I swear I've met myself coming back twice this week already. If you were to ask me why I'm doing this job at all, I'd be hard put to it not to bark back "Good question!"

"Salome! Here, bring a jug of wine for this gentleman, will you? And one for me too, while you're about it. *What?* What d'you mean, 'We've run out'? There were seventeen full casks in the stable store last night. I counted them myself before I finally collapsed into bed, which was well past midnight, I might tell you. Oh my word – do I have to think of everything for everybody round here? If you can't move casks yourself, my dear, get that lazy good-for-nothing Timaeus to do it for you; it's about time he did something to earn his keep for a change."

I'm sorry, forgive me. Here, do sit down. I'm afraid I must be giving you the impression that I'm overstressed. I'm not really – well, not more than normal. But as you can see, we're more than usually busy at the moment. It's this census thing, of course. I must admit, I groaned when I first saw the notices about it posted up round the town – more unnecessary Roman interference in the lives of honest, law-abiding citizens, I thought. On reflection, I realised it might mean more business for the inn – but not for one moment did I suspect it would be as mad as this.

"Yes, Jude, what is it? Oh for goodness' sake, boy – you know perfectly well that we haven't got any rooms; we've been booked solid for days. We'd have to tip the cattle out of the stable to squeeze any more guests in – but then I could hardly charge them the full rate for that, could I? Go and move them on, Jude, will you? Politely, of course. And when you've done that, you can clear that table over there of all

9

those tankards; get them washed and dried, scrub the table-top down, and renew the rushes on the floor. Goodness, is it only me that can see all the jobs crying out to be done in this inn?"

Now, where were we? Ah yes, the census. It's brought people here from all over the country. The Romans can't have had the first idea how much upheaval the whole thing would cause. I hear there's total chaos on the roads, though I have to take other people's word for that – fat chance I have of swanning off to see what's happening, even outside my own front door. As you know, everyone's required to register at their birthplace, which is why at least half the population seems to be on the move. Now, I'm lucky there, of course. I haven't got to go anywhere, though the opportunity'd be a fine thing. The inn's been in my family for I don't know how many generations. There's even folks who'll tell you it's been here in one form or another since the time of King David himself, but I wouldn't know about that. All I can say is that I was born here, and no doubt, I'll die here – and sooner than I'd expect, I should think, if things go on the way they are at the moment.

"Jude, now I ask you: Has anything changed? Has anyone suddenly upped and left? Has a whole new room miraculously sprung out of the ground, complete with furnishings and all? No? Then it's got to be the same answer, hasn't it? We couldn't accommodate a single extra mouse tonight, let alone two more humans. Hold on a minute; did my ears deceive me, or did you actually say she's heavily pregnant? You did? She is? So you're witless enough to come in here and ask if we can take in two more guests, tonight of all nights, when in fact, any minute now there may actually be *three*? What do they think this is, a lying-in hospital or something? Words fail me. Just go and be nice to them – say we're extremely sorry, but we're breaking all the regulations already – risk of fire, sanitary facilities strained to breaking point – and we wouldn't wish to endanger them at this critical time. Say something like that, but just get rid of them."

I'm sorry you had to overhear that. He's my eldest, you know; as nice a boy as you could wish for. But if he's to take over from me eventually, he's got to learn how to handle situations like that – firmly but tactfully, so as not to tarnish our reputation and lose possible future trade. I'd like to think we'll be here as long in the future as we've already been in the past, but the way things are these days, I can't say I feel very confident. Excuse me a minute.

"Martha, you should be in the kitchen, helping your mother get the evening meal ready. The guests'll all be barging in here any minute now, banging on the tables and demanding to be fed. Oh alright, well, get the lamps lit first, then."

It certainly gets dark early this time of year, doesn't it? And I wasn't joking when I spoke about the risk of fire to Jude just then. You watch and see if every single guest doesn't pick up a log and throw it into the grate when he comes in. They all seem to think they can act as if they own the place just because they're paying to be here.

"Jude, I am known throughout this town, and for a good few miles all round it, as a remarkably good-tempered, tolerant, and jovial host; but I think my patience is, at long last, just about beginning to run out. Watch my mouth. We are completely full up. We have no more room anywhere. We cannot accommodate anyone else. Oh, here, out of my way. As usual, if I want anything done properly round here, I must do it myself."

"Good evening, sir, ma'am. How can I help you? Oh, accommodation – I can't tell you how sorry I am, but of all the things I'd love to help you with, that's the one thing I haven't got. No, completely booked up I'm afraid, and all paid for, too. Where are you from? Nazareth, eh? That's way up north, isn't it? You've had quite a journey, then. So how long have you been travelling? Here for the census I suppose, are you? Yes, so's half of the rest of the country, it seems. Well, if this is your family town, haven't you got any relatives here you could stay with? Oh dear, well, friends then, acquaintances, business associates? What's your line, sir? Hmm, yes, I suppose carpenters do tend to have only local contacts. Well, I really do wish I could help, but there simply isn't anything I can do. I know for a fact that practically every house-holder in the town has turned guest-house keeper this week – and some of them haven't hesitated to make a fine old killing out of it, I can tell you. Oh, look out! Oh, poor soul, she nearly fainted clean away then. Yes, of course, I can see – and it looks like her time has come, too. Here, you hold her up on the donkey while I lead him into the yard; at least she won't be jostled there by all these people crowding the street.

"Well, yes, it's our stable, but the animals are in there now, of course. Yes, it's dry, certainly, and reasonably clean. But surely you wouldn't want her to spend the night there, not in the condition she's in? Yes, I see what you mean. Oh, my dear sir, it looks like you don't have a choice now – and neither, it seems, do I. Martha, quick, get your mother out here. Never mind about the evening meal, the guests'll have to fend for themselves for once. There's something far more important happening here, and it's happening right now. Tell her to bring hot water and lots of clean linen. Timaeus, you great oaf, don't just stand there gawping. Get that clean straw there spread out over the floor. Here, help me move this manger first. No, wait, I've had a brainwave: it'll make a perfect cradle for a newborn baby, won't it? Salome – blankets, rugs, woollen cloths – anything you can lay your hands on to make the straw warm and comfy for the lady to lie on. What did you say her name is? Mary – oh, how lovely. That's my sister's name, too. Lamps, Jude, lamps! As many as you can find; we can hardly see what we're doing in here at all, now. Are the animal pens secure? No, leave them where they are. Things have gone too far for us to move them now. Alright, everybody, outside now, if you please. We've done all we can for the time being."

"Can we come in now, please? Oh, it's a boy! Isn't he beautiful? What will you call him? Jesus – that's perfect. Doesn't he look lovely? And how are you, my dear? Are you sure you're alright? You look really radiant. Congratulations, my dear sir – another generation for your family! Who did you say you are descended from? Really? Direct from King David himself? Well, how about that? Jesus – it means Saviour, doesn't it? Born of David's line, born in David's town, born in my stable! I'll remember tonight for the rest of my days."

A Shepherd

People are surprisingly ignorant about shepherds and their work. They tend to look down on us, assuming that we are simple souls who are only doing this job because we are not capable of anything better. Not that that worries me in the slightest; a judgement depends for its validity on the position from which it is made. If political power, social status, religious reputation, and worldly wealth are important to you, then you won't be needing me to advise you not to take up shepherding. But there are other things in life, are there not, such as those intimations of God which come to us through the senses he has given us. Have you ever known the taste of goat's milk still warm from the udder, the feel of a sheepskin coat, the smell of grass after rainfall, the sight of a lamb's tail quivering ecstatically as it urgently works its mother's teat, and above all, the incessant bleating of the flock, blown on the wind from the floor of a valley to the top of a hill?

Of course, I realise that these are all drawn from the major preoccupation of my life – the care of sheep and goats –but you would be very much mistaken if you were to think to yourself that they merely confirm your private opinion that a shepherd's life must be mind-numbingly dull, limited, and boring. In the open emptiness of the hills, I have space and time to be myself. I have opportunities to reflect on things the rabbi taught me in school and on what I learn when the duty roster allows me to get to the synagogue on Sabbath days. I take the theory I hear from others and lay it alongside the facts of my own experience. It will probably come as no great surprise to you to learn that there is often considerable discrepancy between the two.

At first this used to worry me, but I believe I have been saved from the worst excesses of individualism by the moderating influences of the people I work with. For a shepherd's life is, despite outsiders' assumptions, a very balanced one. Obviously, there are times when, in terms of human company, we are wholly on our own, and that is when I think, meditate, and pray. But there are periods when we work together and have ample opportunities to share our thoughts and discuss our ideas. The interplay of these varying experiences has forged for me an understanding of God that has moved on from mere awareness to a living relationship. If that sounds unbearably prim and smug, I can only apologise; all I can say is that it is the best I can do in trying to communicate things which elude expression. The ultimate realities of life are far from being contained or conveyed by mere words.

That is why music means so much to me. From as far back as I can remember, I have been totally captivated by it. I recall standing stock still when I was a very young child, gazing in wonder at my uncle as he produced entrancing sounds from a piece of wood with holes in it. Almost as soon as I could hold one, I learnt to play simple tunes on a pipe; I have since mastered other wind instruments and the harp and lyre. But long spells in the hills when I am on duty with the sheep mean that I can only take my single pipe with me, so of course, I use my voice. It would probably startle travellers if they heard me singing psalms as loudly as I sometimes do. But apart from the occasional camel train moving in slow silhouette along the skyline in the distance or winding down a hillside to camp for the night in a well-watered valley, I rarely see anyone in the Judaean uplands as I move endlessly with my flock in search of pasture.

But please do not think I seek commendation for sensibly making an effort to come to terms with a lonely life simply because I have no choice in the matter. I have, of course, had ample experience of town life in Bethlehem, where I was born and was brought up, and I have also briefly tasted city life. I take it that you are aware that the sheep I herd are no ordinary beasts; they are a very special breed indeed, reared for the highest of purposes. They are destined to be the sacrificial offerings on the altar in the Temple at Jerusalem itself, and from my earliest days, I have been made inescapably aware of the heavy responsibility I bear for making absolutely certain that there are no blemishes of any kind on any of the animals I make available to the Temple authorities. That was how I came to sample city life: three of us young trainee shepherds had to go to Jerusalem for a course of instruction on the priests' requirements for sacrificial beasts – and very exacting requirements they are, too. That was when I encountered the noise and pressure, the bustle and stress, the sharp practice and the underhand dealing that always seem to be generated by so many people living and working so close to each other. And that was also when I decided it was not for me.

Yet again, you must not conclude that my background and upbringing as a country lad predisposed me to a jaundiced view of urban life. I looked forward to my stay in Jerusalem – I had such vivid memories of my visit there when I was twelve years old for my initiation as a son of the Law. The ceremonies involved were suitably impressive to my developing young mind, but they were overshadowed by the effect the music had on me. The singing of the trained choirs in the Temple seemed to my fervent imagination to be as close as human beings could get to the sound of the praise surrounding the very throne of God in heaven. And when all the people crowding the Temple and its courtyards joined in the responses, I was reduced to inexplicable tears by the sheer emotion of participating in the worship of the universe offered to the Holy One of Israel. The combination of the high voices of the choir of boys standing at the foot of the steps leading up to the court of the priests, the thunderous bass of the mass of worshippers thronging the court of Israel, and the spine-tingling thrill of the rams' horns, trumpets, and cymbals all united in giving honour to God, completely melted me. I knew, however briefly, however imperfectly, that I had glimpsed the glory of heaven. I had experienced for myself the breaking through of the presence of the Lord.

That is why I was instantly able to recognise it when I experienced it again. Furthermore, should you require independent corroboration of what I am saying, there are witnesses who can confirm my account of what happened one night last week. Four of us were on duty together on the hills just above Bethlehem. There was an indefinable but very real sense of something special in the air that night. We watched the sun sink slowly behind the hills, seeming curiously larger than it normally does in the daytime, deepening from yellow through orange to red as it set. For an hour or more, the cloudless sky held a palette of changing colours, ranging from palest blue to light green, turquoise, purple, and eventually, of course, black. It was uncommonly cold – there was almost a hint of frost in the air, and everything was utterly still, silent, and expectant. There were a few settling-down sounds from the sheep and an occasional putter of life from the fire we had lit to keep ourselves warm, but as the night closed in on us, even we fell completely silent, strangely aware of a solemn sense of awe all round us. It was almost as if nature itself was holding its breath.

I remember thinking that the stars were shining more brightly than I had ever noticed before, when I became aware of a glow behind me. As I turned round, it strengthened, and I saw a young man dressed in white standing there. The radiance shining from him steadily enveloped

15

all of us, and we cowered in front of him, hiding our faces in our cloaks. His first words urged us not to be afraid, and we plucked up courage to look at him directly. What he then told us made me realise why the night felt so special. It was indeed special. In the simplest of words, he said that that very night, in our own familiar town of Bethlehem, the Messiah had been born. He described him as Saviour and spoke of great joy for all people. He invited us to see for ourselves, telling us to look for a newborn baby, wrapped in swaddling clothes and lying in a manger.

We were still speechless with wonder when the light all round us brightened to a white intensity, and to our utter amazement, we saw a countless host of angels, filling all the sky and making such music as can never have been heard on earth before nor ever can be again. They sang paeans of praise to God in such ravishing harmonies that I felt the same surge of ecstasy as I had known in the Temple all those years before, and I knew with equal certainty that I had been allowed a second foretaste on earth of the indescribable glory of the worship offered in heaven.

It was only as my eyes began to recognise the familiar shapes of resting sheep that I realised that the vision was fading, and the sound of singing was moving further and further away. We gaped at each other, immobile for a split second. And then my three colleagues were all up on their feet, simultaneously gabbling excitedly. Almost before I realized what was happening, they had gone, and I was left alone to guard the sheep and tend the fire.

The first light of dawn was already picking out the line of hills to the east when they eventually returned. They said they had run all the way down to the town and had had no trouble in finding the baby. He had been born in the stable behind the inn and was sleeping peacefully in the warmth and safety of a manger by the time they had arrived. They remarked that it looked as if I had not moved for the whole of the time they had been away. I probably had not – my whole being was still completely absorbed in the song the angels had sung: "Glory to God in the highest, and on earth, peace, goodwill towards men."

A Wise Man

Kingship seems to be a remarkably elastic concept. My own understanding of it was initially fashioned by the influences of my birth and upbringing. As I grew up, the tutors my father engaged for me introduced me to the teachings of Plato, specifically his fine idea that fitness to rule should depend on wisdom, acquired through education and proved in practice, rather than on the mere fact of inheritance or the accident of birth. It was entirely natural that I should be exposed to such ideas; my homeland east of the Arabian Desert has been steeped in Greek culture and thought ever since Alexander the Great's conquest of most of the ancient world more than three centuries ago. Of course, Greek soldiers have long since gone, but Greek ideas, Greek civilisation, and above all, the Greek language, made a lasting impact, and they are still very much with us today.

And yet they have only overlaid the characteristics of our earlier culture; they have not uprooted or replaced them. I am aware that I have inherited many of the attitudes and values of the ancient civilisations of the Tigris and Euphrates valleys, and I can often identify survivals of Babylonian and Mesopotamian beliefs and practices among my subjects. Indeed, I deliberately cultivate some of those characteristics myself. For instance, from my earliest years I have been captivated by the mystery of the sky at night. In the flat, featureless landscape here on the very edge of the desert, the vast dome of the sky dominates our life both by day and by night – but especially by night. In the clear and cloudless air, the stars shine more brightly than polished jewels set in deep velvet, but they are also much more than just objects of great beauty.

I am conscious that I am heir to at least two strands of belief about the stars: one deriving from traditional folklore tales that identify them with the gods and their activities, and another, based on scientific study, which regards them as natural objects, with us a part of the one physical universe. I would quite understand if I were charged with being unable to distinguish between the impacts of these two different philosophies on my own attitudes, but I would vigorously rebut any accusation that my approach to the mystery of the stars is in any way tainted with

17

the foolishness of astrology. Many years ago, I was presented with a copy of the sacred writings of the Jewish religion, and I read them with a growing sense of wonder at their exalted conception of God. I still frequently turn to them when I am wearied by the naivety of the religious beliefs and practices of my people, and I base my theory of the stars on a striking passage I came across in the Book of Psalms:

"The heavens are telling the glory of God,
And the firmament proclaims His handiwork.
Day to day pours forth speech,
And night to night declares knowledge.
There is no speech, nor are there words;
Their voice is not heard:
Yet their voice goes out through all the earth,
And their words to the end of the world."

This perception of the stars as the messengers of God is far more satisfying to my intellect than any of the other views currently in circulation; it provides me with a convincing justification of the worthwhileness of the activity I have always regarded as an enjoyable and suitable pastime for a philosopher king.

So I continue to study the night sky with unabated intensity. But I do not do so on my own. Balthazar and Melchior, rulers of the states to the north and south respectively of my own kingdom, both share my fascination with the stars, and we communicate regularly with each other on this, as on other matters of common interest. My own astronomer royal is, of course, assisted by a small team of trained and skilled observers. You may well therefore imagine the excitement caused when one of the assistant astronomers reported that he seemed to have detected a heavenly body which none of us had noticed before. I joined the team outside straightaway, and we all agreed that this was indeed something new. We had observed three conjunctions of the two largest planets only two years previously and therefore knew perfectly well that this phenomenon was of an entirely different nature.

I immediately despatched messengers on fast horses to my two neighbouring sovereigns, only to receive emissaries from both of them with identical messages: they had also seen the new star and were as intrigued by it as I was. I followed up my initial communications with invitations to Balthazar and Melchior to visit me, so that we could share our thoughts and theories on this unexpected appearance. While

I waited for them to arrive, I spent almost the whole of every night on the roof of my palace, unable to tear my eyes away from the astonishing sight presented to them. The new star grew dramatically in brilliance; in a matter of only a few nights, it came to outshine all the other objects in the sky (these were moonless nights). It was an object of quite breathtaking beauty, like a diamond of rarest purity. The intensity of its brightness made it seem as if it were much closer than all the other stars, and I felt an irrational desire to reach out and pluck it, as one does fruit from a tree.

As soon as my brother monarchs arrived, it was obvious that they were as deeply affected by this development in the heavens as I was. We debated it earnestly and quickly concluded that its unprecedented character demanded that it be interpreted as a sign given by God to announce a unique happening on earth. As the star was positioned due west of us, we had no difficulty in agreeing that it indicated a special event in the Roman province of Judaea, since the first five hundred miles or so in that direction consists solely of barren desert. In what I now realise must have seemed to our servants to be little short of a boyish rush of enthusiasm, we ordered preparations to be made immediately for a joint state visit to Jerusalem. On a sudden impulse, I took with me my copy of the Jewish sacred writings. In the course of our journey, I dipped into it with increasing interest as I realised that the Jews had nurtured a centuries-old longing for a deliverer to free them from all their troubles.

Of our journey westwards, I will say nothing other than it took longer than we expected it would, and it was fraught with unforeseen difficulties, petty problems, irritating incidents, and annoying accidents. Most disconcerting of all, however, was the fact that although it never completely disappeared, the star which was the cause of all these troubles dimmed alarmingly – a fact which did not pass unnoticed among the members of our retinues. Their discontent became daily more evident, but it was effectively dissipated when we finally breasted the last ridge of the Judaean hills and caught our first glimpse of Jerusalem, serene in the morning sunlight, and crowned with the splendid golden dome of its magnificent Temple.

Closer acquaintance with the city hugely moderated our initial favourable impressions. The streets were narrow and crowded, the people dirty and suspicious, the Roman occupying power disrespectful and unhelpful, and the religious authorities disdainful and condescending.

Before the day was out we were received by King Herod. All three of us took an instant dislike to him, and we were immediately able to credit the tales of his cruelty and treachery which had long filtered through to us back at home. Moreover, we were greatly taken aback to discover that neither he nor anyone else in Jerusalem knew anything about a newborn king of the Jews. He showed an interest in our mission that was more than merely polite and went to the trouble of ordering his religious experts to give us the full benefit of all their knowledge on the subject of their long-awaited Messiah. As a result, we found ourselves on the road to the little town of Bethlehem, less than three miles south of the city.

We were astonished by the meanness and poverty of the place but were vastly reassured by a sudden surge in the brilliance of the star. It was now visible well before dusk each evening and long after dawn each morning. The town was small enough for the wide-eyed inhabitants to have no difficulty in directing us to a little house occupied by a couple who had a baby who was one year old – which was exactly the time that had elapsed since we first saw the new star in the sky. We stooped to enter through the low doorway and knew immediately that we had found the object of our journey. Each of us instinctively took from our servants' hands the presents we had brought for a king and laid them on the mud floor in front of the child on his mother's knee. We knelt in silent homage.

After a restless night of strange dreams in the wretchedly uncomfortable village inn, we started on the direct route home, travelling due east, without calling again on Herod in Jerusalem. I mused to myself during the journey on the differences between my own kingship, the kingship of Herod of Judaea, and the kingship of Jesus.

SIMEON

Lord, I am tired – very, very tired – and my tiredness is not assuaged by sleep. I am not short of sleep; in your bounty, you give me freely of your precious gift of sleep, but every morning when I wake I feel no more refreshed than when I went to bed at night. This is no surprise to me. I know full well it is the fruit of age, so I do not complain. You have been very gracious to me, Lord. You have blessed me with long life and good health, and though I now am weak, I have been strong. I recall my youth with gratitude, and thank you that you blessed me with the pleasures of physical vigour. I acknowledge that I have lacked nothing throughout all my life in this holy city of Jerusalem, the place you chose so long ago for your dwelling among men. You have given me food and drink, clothing and shelter, and honour and respect among the devout who fear your name and seek your face. I have not sought deferential greetings in the streets, the best seats at feasts, or the chief place in the synagogue, yet all these you have granted me. Though the Gentile has sullied our streets, defiled our daughters, and profaned the precincts of your house, nevertheless you have preserved inviolate the sanctity of your sanctuary. So I daily prostrate myself before you for the privilege of worshipping you in this, your holy house, and of communing with the righteous remnant who earnestly seek the consolation of Israel.

But Lord, how long will it be before you heed the prayers of your faithful ones? You have promised me that I shall not taste death until I have seen your Messiah; but the years have gone by, and I am now old and tired – very, very tired. It cannot be long now before I shall be gathered to my fathers and go down into the darkness of death. When will you fulfil your word to your servant? You have tested me almost as much as you tested our forefather Abraham. I cannot hold to your promise unless you give me the same faith as you gave him. I sit here day by day in my accustomed place in Solomon's Porch, and I watch the endless stream of people passing by. I wonder: How will you fulfil your promise to me? How shall I recognise the Messiah when he comes? Will there be soldiers on horseback? Shall I hear trumpets and drums, and the distant sound of people cheering? Will your chosen one be a strong young man dressed in white with flashing eyes, branding aloft his naked sword? Will we be irresistibly drawn to him by the promise of power, wealth, and victory over our enemies? What will be your sign, Lord? How shall I know?

And still they stream past me – Jews and Gentiles, men and women, young and old, swarthy Arabs, dark-skinned Africans, handsome Greeks, proud Romans, pilgrims from Galilee, and my neighbours and friends here in Jerusalem – a seemingly unending tide of humanity. Some are merely curious, many are clearly undertaking a dutiful enactment of ritual, a few – a very, very few – obviously are deeply moved by being in the very courts of the house of the living God. I watch them as they move slowly by, chattering excitedly to each other, pointing to the splendid workmanship of the huge stones of the Temple building, white and brilliant in the golden sunlight.

Of course, I remember the previous Temple. Earliest experiences make the deepest and longest-lasting impressions. I inevitably have fond memories of the old building, because it was the backdrop to my formative years. This present Temple complex is certainly larger and much grander than the old one, but it still seems brash and new to me, and it has unfortunately given considerably greater scope to hard-nosed commercial men. One side of the colonnade, where I am sitting now, is completely taken up with traders' stalls and currency booths. Lord, I am uneasy about this growing trend. Of course your worshippers must not offer blemished sacrifices, but the cacophony of caged doves and pigeons, the bleating and lowing of tethered sheep and cattle, and the calls and arguments of traders and money-changers penetrate even the court of Israel and insinuate themselves into the worship of your people. Is this really what you require? Can this be pleasing to you? I see sharp-dealing city slickers defrauding trusting country people, and I recall your prophet's words: "He has shown you, O man, what is good; and what does the Lord require of you, but to do justly, to love mercy, and to walk humbly with your God." I grieve that this people's heart is not right with you. We honour you outwardly, but our deeds negate our protestations of faith.

In my more sanguine moments, I realise that despite the deference traditionally shown in our culture to the aged, the young know that the future belongs to them. I see their eager faces in the crowd, their bright eyes, their happy smiles, their unlined brows, and their unbowed backs, and I feel a pang of nostalgia for youth – my own youth, so unconcerned and carefree, now so long-lost and irrecoverable – and my failing heart warms to the glow of the rising generation. This young woman in the crowd, for instance, is typical of the glory of our past and the hope of our future. She has a baby in her arms and her husband, clearly older than she is, at her side. They are walking more slowly than the throng all around them. She has caught my eye – I struggle to my feet. She stops. Why am I moving towards her? Her husband carries a wickerwork cage holding two doves. Clearly, they are on their way to present their baby to you, Lord, so he must be their first son. I look into her face, and, prompted by an impulse from entirely outside of myself, I ask, "Can I hold him?" She turns enquiringly to her husband; he nods, and she places this tiny perfect form in my arms.

Suddenly, I know. This is he – he whom you have promised, he whom prophets have foretold and priests have awaited, he whom kings have sought and the people have longed for. At long last, you have kept your word to your servant – you have opened my eyes to see and recognise your supreme gift to your creation. Not in the guarded seclusion of a palace throne room, nor in the tight security of a military barracks, but here, in the heart of the mass of humanity swirling all around us, you have unveiled your final and greatest revelation of yourself – a revelation for all peoples, throughout the whole of space and time. You have completed your centuries-old dealings with your chosen people; you have crowned our history with the incomparable glory of the gift of yourself to us in this little child. Now, Lord, I am totally fulfilled. All my weariness has gone. I await your call in utter peace.

The baby is opening his eyes, and I become aware that people have stopped to see what is going on, obstructing the flow of the ceaseless tide of sightseers, but you are giving me a prophecy, and your spirit impels me to speak.

"I bless you in the name of the Lord, who has himself blessed you with this child. Your baby will be as a shepherd to our people, dividing sheep from goats. Many will be offended by him, and, O my dear, you will be pierced as by a sword because of him. All will judge themselves by the way they react to him."

Now my eyes are filling with tears, and my arms begin to tremble as though the innocent child they are holding were bearing the weight of all the woes of the world. I give him back to his mother, and almost blinded by my tears, I turn and stumble as I seek my chair again. I am steadied by a light touch on my arm, and I recognise the lined and wizened face of Phanuel's daughter, Anna. She is quite a lot older than I am, but her energy is not in the least abated, and her faith seems to grow stronger as her age increases. She shames us all with the depth of her devotion. Not a day passes without her being seen here in the Temple, either praying privately or joining in the praises of the worshippers at the times of the morning and evening sacrifices. Above the hubbub of the people babbling all around, I hear her speaking to me.

"I saw and heard everything," she is saying. "The spirit of God was never more clearly present than when you held the child and spoke about him. I saw with my own eyes and heard with my own ears. Now I know that the Messiah is among us. This is a day of good news – we cannot keep it to ourselves. I will tell all the faithful throughout the city that our prayers are answered, our hopes are met, our faith is honoured. Praise be to God!"

Before I can answer, she is gone. I briefly glimpse her diminutive figure scuttling through the crowds with the determined purposefulness of unshakeable certainty. Exhausted, I sit down. How I envy Anna's unquenchable enthusiasm – and her mobility! But then I reflect that in your bounty you give a vast variety of gifts to your servants, and I am grateful for inner peace, for the tranquillity that results from trust, and for the quiet confidence you have given me. So, when your last call comes, serene and clear, calm may my answer be, "Lord, I am here."

HEROD THE GREAT

Allow me to introduce my Grand Vizier, Manahem. Do you not agree that I have good reason to be vastly pleased with myself, Manahem? Yet another birthday has arrived, and I am still king in Jerusalem. Today we will celebrate more than forty years of my recognition by Rome as the rightful ruler of Judaea as well as the all-important anniversary of my birth. Do you still remember that day all those years ago, when I was still only a schoolboy, but you predicted that I would one day be king?

What's that? I know perfectly well that I have not always been accorded the title of king, but what's in a name? Position, power, and prestige are what matter, not empty words. You do realise, don't you, Manahem, that coming from anyone else, those words of yours just then would have resulted in instant imprisonment and early execution. Do not presume upon my goodwill towards you, old friend. I would remind you that I have treated you and your Essene community with favour all these years solely because your prediction came true, but precisely because it came true, what I have given, I can take away.

And do not be so foolish as to think that you could save your miserable old skin by appealing to Rome; remember that I have always had the foresight to remain in favour with Rome, no matter which faction was currently in power there. I have been astute enough to ensure that ever since my father made me governor of Galilee when I was only twenty-five, I have sat in the seat of authority and wielded the sceptre of power.

Ho, there! Summon the scribes: let them record again my triumphs over all my trials and tribulations so that posterity may know and marvel. When the ever-expanding dominion of the Romans clashed with the Parthian power, I prudently ingratiated myself with Mark Antony. He accordingly promoted my interest in the Roman Senate. My successful prosecution of war against the Parthians and Antigonus, that pathetic last remnant of the upstart Maccabaean family, saw me advance from being tetrarch of Galilee to King of Judaea – a dignity, I may say, that could hardly be denied me when I actually captured Jerusalem over thirty years ago.

Manahem, is my remarkable brain playing a trick on me, or do you also sense more noise and commotion than usual in the city today? Have somebody go out and report back, will you? If I find out that there is discontent coming to a head in revolt, I will have my entire secret intelligence service beheaded for incompetence before the night is over – indeed, I will have it done in any case, on suspicion of disloyalty. They are more than likely guilty of complicity in some sort of criminal plot against my royal person.

Now, where was I? Ah, yes, the Parthian Wars. I cannot pretend that I was inconsolably distressed when two of my three brothers were killed in the fighting – their deaths proved to be ideally timed in the interest of smoothing my path to unchallenged power. My third brother has been more of a problem. Despite all my kindness to him – I acquiesced in his being made a partner of my throne, with the title of tetrarch and the enjoyment of the revenue accruing from the whole of the kingdom east of the Jordan – I have had to have him under close surveillance. More than once, it has been reported to me that he was plotting to have me assassinated. It was fortunate for him that death has just carried him off, as I had only recently decided that he must stand trial to answer with his life for the base ingratitude with which he repaid all those years of my kindness and consideration. Fortunately, my sister Salome has been less of a worry to me. Of course, I know perfectly well that she has regularly plotted against other members of my family, but my spies have never had reason to suspect her of treachery against myself.

Is that so? Did you hear that, Manahem? So, my senses did not deceive me; there is extra excitement in the streets today, but not, apparently, arising from any unrest among my loyal subjects. The news is that three princes from states east of the desert have arrived in the city in what sounds like unnecessarily showy pomp. Why was I not told about this beforehand? Have the chief of the intelligence service arrested immediately and executed at dawn for failing to alert me to this development. What do these foreigners want, do you think? Have they come to propose a treaty of alliance – against Parthia, perhaps? Given the high standing of my reputation, that would be perfectly understandable, but I shall have to take into account the likely reaction of the Romans to the idea.

What? They are looking for the newborn king of the Jews? They have come here to worship him? What dastardly conspiracy is this? *I* am the only king of the Jews, and I will remain so. Who is behind this?

They shall not live out this day, whoever they are. I have survived more than thirty years of cynically self-seeking plots against me by my false and faithless family; do they think they can prevail against me now? Mariamne and our two boys, her brother, her grandfather, and even my own firstborn son, Antipater, I have been cruelly compelled to execute for high treason. Whom must I now suspect of seeking to supplant me with, of all things, a newborn baby? Whoever it is, is clearly bent on self-destruction – nobody challenges me and lives. Blood will flow for this. You mark my words, Manahem: torrents of blood will flow.

Eh? Speak up, man. Why have you taken to mumbling inaudibly in your old age? What? Oh. Yes, I see. Hmm, it might be a good idea. Squeeze as much information out of them as possible in the hope that they will incriminate the guilty parties. Alright, then, arrange for them to be contacted and invited here, will you?

Ah, Your Excellencies, greetings to each of you, and welcome to my palace and capital city. Pray enter, and do me the honour to be seated. Attendance within! Let refreshments be offered to our distinguished visitors. I could almost reproach you, Your Excellencies, for not having notified me in advance of your intention to come here so that I could have prepared an even more sumptuous welcome for you. But may I enquire as to the purpose of your visit?

How absolutely fascinating. I cannot say that my own astronomers have reported anything out of the ordinary in the heavens; but perhaps even more disappointing from your point of view, neither has there been a recent birth in my family. In any case, I have only just amended my will again, and the succession is firmly settled on my son Archelaus. But could it be that your quest relates to the religious leader my people have so long expected, the Messiah? Allow me to summon our leading experts in these matters; maybe they will be able to shed some light on this for you. Oh no, I assure you it will be no trouble at all. I shall be most interested to hear what they have to say about it.

Well, Your Excellencies, you heard their conclusion. I am sorry we are not able to satisfy your intentions here, but I am pleased to say that Bethlehem is less than three miles south of the city. It will seem as nothing compared to the hundreds of miles you have already covered. Oh, and I beg that you will be so gracious as to visit me again as soon as you have located the object of your search. It is most exciting to learn that the Messiah has been born in my reign. I shall naturally wish to hasten to pay him my own respects, so I shall be most grateful if you will kindly return to tell me exactly where I may find him.

Manahem, I grow more uneasy by the day. It is now nearly a month since those over-dressed, self-important posturers arrived here unannounced with their totally unconvincing claim of wanting to pay homage to a newborn king. What lies behind it, Manahem? In the cold light of day, I wonder if they were playing out an elaborate charade to spy on us. Is it even possible that the Parthians are behind it all? But at night, I cannot sleep for fear that I am under threat from a scarcely weaned infant. Manahem, organise an undercover enquiry to find out if three exotic easterners on camels, with a whole caravan of attendants, have actually shown up in Bethlehem in the last few weeks. They can hardly have gone unnoticed in that dead-and-alive little place, can they?

They did? So where are they now? Already far into the desert on their way home, are they? I see; then I shall not waste time or effort on flamboyant or useless gestures. I shall strike at the very heart of this threat. How long ago was it that this famous star of theirs was first alleged to have appeared? Eighteen months, wasn't it? Right. Summon the army commander-in-chief. Every male child under the age of two in Bethlehem and its vicinity is to be eliminated this very night; not one is to escape. Take note, Manahem, how true I am to my word. Did I not say that torrents of blood would flow because of this event? History will assuredly applaud my action. Indeed, the unswerving consistency of all my deeds could well justify me being called Herod the Great.

Just like Us
II. Round the Cross

Judas Iscariot

It all seemed such a good idea at first – more than a good idea, much more.

Like most teenagers, I suppose, I was an idealist. I passionately hated the occupying power. One of my earliest memories of the little synagogue school at Kerioth was of the old rabbi who taught us boys there, endlessly reminding us that we Jews were God's chosen people. It was a lesson I learnt well – so well, that I have never been able to come to terms with the fact that we are under the heel of Gentile rulers. I grappled desperately with an impossible problem: the God who had miraculously fulfilled his promise to our ancestor Abraham that he would make a great nation of his descendants, now seemed to have forgotten the people he had chosen. It was no help to be told by well-meaning but unintelligent scribes that it had all happened before, many times. They were apparently quite unable to see that there were no parallels between, for example, the catastrophe of the deportation to Babylon nearly six hundred years ago and the calamity of our present subjection to Roman rule. The Scriptures clearly teach that our forefathers richly deserved the disasters which fell upon them. Stubbornly ignoring ample warnings from the long line of prophets, they had sinned greatly by turning away from God and plunging headlong into the shameful worship of the idols of the peoples around them.

The contrast with our own situation could hardly be greater. There has rarely, if ever, been a more profound commitment to our religion than there is now. It seems as if our generation has, at long last, learnt the lessons so faithfully proclaimed by the prophets. The intensity of our devotion can be measured by the number and strength of our religious parties, from tolerant Sadducees to exclusive Pharisees. We are meticulous about every last detail of our religious observances, from the payment of a tithe of all our produce, through the careful observance of a whole raft of rules relating to the Sabbath, to the ritual washing of cups and bowls and the hands that will use them. We have a nationwide network of scribes and rabbis teaching the Law in synagogues in every town and village, and we have an impressive hierarchy of academics, Levites, and priests maintaining an unbroken system of sacrifices in Jerusalem to ensure God's favour by scrupulous obedience to all his laws. Even King Herod, that hated Idumaean forced on us by the occupying power, sensed the strength of our contemporary religious sentiment. He tried to curry favour with his unwilling subjects by building an admittedly splendid third Temple in Jerusalem as an expression of the depth of our spiritual feeling.

But there is more to it than just the formal commitment of the official establishment, thorough-going though that is. The visible externals of our faith are only the surface expressions of a deep underlying religious sensitivity, which is now felt by virtually the whole nation. In my own lifetime, there has developed a feeling of expectancy which has run like a flame through all our people – the expectancy that God is about to fulfil, at long last, his final and greatest promise of a Messiah to deliver us from all our enemies and to set us up as rulers of all the world, in a kingdom which will far surpass in power and extent even the mighty Roman Empire. There is an ever-widening feeling that the depth of our present political misfortunes, combined as it is with the unprecedented height of our religious fervour, has created the perfect atmosphere for the coming of the Messiah.

This conviction was brought home to me as a lad as my father told me of the appearance in recent years, first of Theudas and then of Judas the Galilaean, both of whom seemed for a brief while as if they might be the long-awaited anointed one. As it turned out, of course, neither of them was, but their emergence only increased the speculation that the coming of the true Messiah was imminent, and I, at any rate, was more than half-prepared when I first met Jesus of Nazareth, nearly three years ago now. True, his emphasis on purely spiritual values, such as repentance, faith, and love, was unexpected, even a mite disappointing, but I was reassured when he invited men like Simon the Zealot, a member of an extremist revolutionary party, and that financially astute inland revenue officer Matthew to join his little band of associates. My confidence in him was confirmed when he asked me to act as treasurer to his group. True, there wasn't a great deal to do. I only needed one small bag to carry all the money that came in to support thirteen of us full-time, and I was considerably embarrassed when he had to borrow a coin from someone in the crowd to illustrate his reply when he was asked whether or not it was right to pay taxes to the Romans. On the other hand, I was very impressed when he met the demand for the Temple tax by simply telling Peter to go fishing and to open the mouth of the first fish he caught – there was a silver coin inside which paid the tax for both of them.

There were other miracles, too – lots of them – and although Jesus's teaching caused considerable surprise and raised a lot of doubts as to whether he could really be the Messiah we were expecting, his campaign seemed to chime in perfectly with the public mood. His initial success in Galilee was exhilarating. I was little short of intoxicated by the sudden prestige I acquired as a member of his closest circle of associates. There were sometimes seemingly endless queues of people, some of them quite important, asking me to put in a special request for him to do them a favour – usually to cure an ill or disabled relative or friend. It seemed positively ungracious to refuse the financial inducements they often persisted in pressing into my hands.

Of course, there was suspicion of Jesus among the religious establishment. Every time we went south to Jerusalem, we sensed a degree of official disapproval, which increasingly bordered on hostility. But last Sunday, we appeared to have overcome that. Jesus made a dramatic appeal to the capital city and seemed to have succeeded. Although he could only find a donkey to ride on, he let us generate as much excitement as we could, and our enthusiasm spread like wildfire. Crowds of people joined in, cutting branches from the palm trees to wave to and fro and laying their cloaks on the ground in the donkey's path while they shouted excitedly about the coming king. More people streamed out from Jerusalem to meet us, and we all felt we were at last making an impact no one could ignore. However, I personally felt Jesus overreached himself when he let his principles get the better of him in the Temple area. He launched a one-man attack on the traders and money changers in the courtyards, tipping over their tables, opening the bird cages, and, most shocking of all, recklessly sweeping away all their carefully counted piles of coins.

His action seemed to throw away in one foolish move all the advantage he had gained from his triumphal entry earlier in the day. Certainly, the enthusiasm which that had generated drained away rapidly over the next two days, and my own disillusionment was completed when he calmly allowed Martha's sister Mary to pour a bottle of very expensive perfume all over his feet. I was sure he would agree with me when I protested that instead of being wasted like that, the perfume should have been sold, and the proceeds given to the poor. But all I got for my thoughtfulness was a public rebuke. It was that which pushed me into taking the biggest risk of all. I decided I would force Jesus's hand by putting him into a position which would compel him to act against his domestic enemies and sweep him on to raise the standard of revolt against the Romans. I took a very deep breath indeed and informed a Sanhedrin official that I had a proposition to make which might be of interest. I was ushered in to a secret meeting with some of the chief priests, and I offered to lead them to Jesus under cover of darkness, if possible before the Passover Festival though this was now only two days away. They offered me thirty pieces of silver – more money than I had had for the whole of the three years I had given to Jesus.

Straightaway, a golden opportunity presented itself. At our Passover supper last night, Jesus revealed a premonition that he would be betrayed. I broke out into a cold sweat – did he know all about my arrangement with the Sanhedrin? If he did, had he laid plans of his own for frustrating mine? In my rapidly rising panic, I could see the thirty pieces of silver slipping out of my grasp. Where I was trying to force his hand, I now felt that, whether deliberately or not, he was forcing mine. I managed to retain my composure, even to the extent of joining in the chorus of bewildered questions the other eleven were all asking, and then, almost as if in a dream, Jesus slowly turned to me and quietly said, "Do quickly what you have to do." I could scarcely believe my luck. I got up and left the room, half-wondering whether anyone would try to stop me, but no-one did, and I reached the Temple area without any trouble. In no time at all, a detachment of the Temple guard was called out, and I led them to the Garden of Gethsemane, where the thirteen us often spent the night. Sure enough, there they were, and I greeted Jesus in the usual way. There was a short exchange of words; and my heart leaped into my mouth when Jesus said that he could call on the aid of more than twelve legions of angels. This was the moment I had planned for: now, surely, he would use his full powers to restore the kingdom to Israel. But all that ensued was a minor scuffle, after which he actually healed the only man who had suffered a wound, which was a slight one at that. Then he let himself be handcuffed and led away under guard. My mind was reeling – surely he was not going to let slip this ideal opportunity of seizing power for himself and setting us up as judges of the twelve tribes of Israel, as he had once so blithely promised?

Needless to say, I have not slept a wink all night. The gossip in the back streets and bazaars this morning could not be worse. Apparently, the Sanhedrin, in a strictly speaking illegal night-time trial, have found Jesus guilty of blasphemy and are at this very moment demanding the death sentence from the Roman governor. The whole thing has gone hideously wrong. I can scarcely drag myself along because of the weight of the thirty pieces of silver in my belt bag: my head is bursting, my mind is falling apart, my whole life is collapsing about me. And all the time, ringing in my ears are the words from the Psalms I learnt as a boy, all those years ago:

"It is you, my equal, my companion, my familiar friend,
With whom I kept pleasant company;
We walked in the house of God with the throng."

What shall I do? What *can* I do? There is only one thing left for me to do.

SIMON PETER

I've heard it said that your character can be influenced by your surroundings. I'm sure I don't know about such things, but people who know me say they can easily tell I'm a fisherman, quite apart from the smell. Take the wife's mother, for instance; she swears the lake and its moods have gone a long way to making me the man I am. As far as I can tell, I'm just a straightforward, no-nonsense, uncomplicated sort of a bloke. I get on well with open, honest, practical people, and I like to think it's because that's the kind of person I am myself. But I suppose, if I stop to think about it, I could be deceiving myself a bit. Actually, I think I've changed quite a lot in the last three years. Before then, life seemed to be more or less pretty plain sailing. Of course, it had its ups and downs, but my brother and I had worked hard to build up a decent living from fishing on the lake, and when we went into partnership with old Zebedee and his boys James and John, the business went well enough for me to take the plunge and get married. I naturally thought that life would just continue to move along smoothly, with my days filled with nothing more disturbing than worries about boats and nets, the size of catches, and the price I could get for them. But I had reckoned without Jesus.

It all started as calmly as a spring day by the lake — in fact it was a spring day with Galilee at its loveliest: blue sky, warm sunshine, not a cloud in sight, a gentle breeze barely ruffling the surface of the water, and flowers everywhere, as thick as a carpet. Andrew and I were working the inshore water with casting nets when Jesus came along the beach. Of course, we'd heard a lot about him already. Who hadn't? His preaching and teaching had set tongues buzzing all round Capernaum, and from listening to him in the synagogue and talking to him afterwards, we felt we'd got to know him a bit.

But it came as a complete bolt from the blue when on this particular morning he just looked us both straight in the eye and simply said, "Follow me." Yet I knew immediately he meant exactly what he said, and d'you know, we did just that. We stowed the casting nets in the boat and walked along the beach with him, and we've been walking along with him ever since. Until last night, that is – but more of that in a minute.

I've described my moment of decision about Jesus in that much detail, because it was the most astounding thing that ever happened in my life – or is ever likely to happen, whatever the future may bring. Yet it was so undramatic, so quiet, so, sort of, almost normal. Once or twice, when I've looked back and thought about it, I've idly wondered whether I was completely mad to do what I did, but I've never regretted it. What would *you* have done in the circumstances? It was a totally unavoidable challenge to choose between two options – and yet there was really no alternative. I remember Jesus saying on a later occasion, "Whoever is not with me is against me," so not deciding would have been making a decision just as much as was the response we did in fact make.

I never had the faintest idea what would be the result of that quiet encounter on that lovely spring morning almost exactly three years ago. Jesus has turned my life inside out and upside down – or perhaps I should say, right way up. He is at one and the same time, the most unsettling and yet the most reassuring person I have ever met. He has more than once driven me from adoration to desperation and back again. There was that time soon after he first called us to follow him full-time: he'd just begun to make a deep impression himself and to catch a great deal more than merely local attention, when, as if to bring the lesson home to us, he said to me, "Put out into the deep water, and let down your nets for a catch." After a fruitless night's hard work on the lake, I was exasperated by this carpenter from the hills telling me, a life-long fisherman, how to do my trade. But just in time I remembered the wife ticking me off for my temper – she's had to do it often enough, in all conscience – so I checked myself and did as he said. I swear, we've never had such a catch, before or since. A wave of emotion surged over me, and I just fell to my knees in front of him and begged him to leave me – I somehow felt both judged and condemned by the spiritual power of the man.

I experienced the same feeling quite a while later, when Jesus took three of us on a mountain-walking holiday. It was a cloudless day in early summer when we reached the snow line; I was panting heavily from the steep climb and feeling faint from the thinness of the air at that height, when John suddenly grabbed my arm and motioned me to look at Jesus. He was a little ahead of us and had turned to face us. There was a brilliance about him which made the brightness of the sunlight and the snow positively grey by comparison, and as we watched open-mouthed with amazement, two other men – we had no problem in recognising them as Moses and Elijah – walked into the glory surrounding him, greeted him like old friends, and chatted away with him as if they had known him for ages. Out of the corner of my eye, I could see mountain mists rolling down towards us. Terrified that we would lose sight of the three of them, I blurted out something wildly unrealistic about building three little mountain huts as shelters for them. Then the mist closed in on us, and for the second time since we had been with him, we heard a voice, which we had no choice but to accept as the voice of God, saying, "This is my beloved Son; with him I am well pleased." We fell to the ground, petrified, until we felt a hand on our shoulders. There was Jesus, on his own, looking no different from what he always did.

That was the culmination of a week which brought me swings of experience as sudden and extreme as changes in conditions on the lake. Only six days previously, as we were trekking into the foothills of the mountains north of Galilee, Jesus had revealed an intriguing curiosity to know what people were saying about him. We duly passed on the comments we had heard.

Suddenly, he sharpened the question dramatically by asking us who we thought he was. Well, of course, all twelve of us had chewed it over with each other for more than two years, and I knew I was speaking for all of us when I said, "You are the Messiah, the Son of the Living God." He seized on that eagerly, and said something to me, which made me feel simultaneously highly elated, and deeply humbled: "Blessed are you, Simon son of Jonah! For flesh and blood have not revealed this to you, but my Father in heaven."

Then he went on to say that we were going to Jerusalem, and with a sad, distant look in his eyes, he spoke about rejection, suffering, and death. I felt that his words of only a few minutes earlier gave me the right to say something, so I began to protest against this defeatist talk. I was totally unable to believe the evidence of my senses when he suddenly turned on me, his dark eyes blazing with a mix of fear and anger, and told me to get out of his sight; he accused me of thinking like men, not like God – and unbelievably, he actually called me Satan. The others all said I went white with shock, and I can tell you, I nursed the hurt of that for days.

Which brings me to last night. I said earlier I would come back to it, didn't I? Well, at our Passover supper in young Mark's mother's house, I got another bad shock. Towards the end of a long and very sombre after-dinner talk, Jesus suddenly warned us that Satan (see? that name again) had been given permission to test us. Then he looked directly at me and said, "But I have prayed for you, that your own faith may not fail."

I was so taken aback that, for once, I hardly knew what to say, but I mumbled something about being ready to go with him to prison and death. Then he really devastated me. He said, "I tell you, Peter, the cock will not crow this day until you have denied three times that you know me."

I protested passionately, "Even though I must die with you, I will not deny you."

But now, barely twenty-four hours later, it has all happened – don't ask me how. The storm of thoughts, emotions, and feelings raging in me today is far more violent than the most furious squall I ever encountered on the lake. There is a confused blur in my mind of flaring lights in the Garden of Gethsemane, armed men shouting, and Jesus being hustled off to the high priest's palace. John and I stumbled after him in the dark, and because he knows someone on Caiaphas's staff, John was able to get me past the guard on the gate and into the courtyard.

It was the worst possible thing that could have happened: I was immediately recognised and accused of being one of Jesus's followers. To my utter horror, I heard myself denying it; but I was still sweating with fear when some of the people warming themselves round the fire said I was one of the prisoner's disciples. My mouth dry with terror, I denied it again; but then a relative of the man whose ear I had sliced off during the brief struggle in the garden when Jesus was arrested, insisted that he had seen me there. I panicked completely and swore blind that I had never known the man. To my unspeakable relief, the group round the fire let the matter drop, and the conversation moved on to something else. As casually as I could manage, I began to move too, away from the firelight, and towards the gate; but I was stopped dead in my tracks. The cock crowed, and at that very moment, Jesus was being taken across the courtyard. For the second time that night, he looked directly at me. His words at supper just a few hours previously flooded back into my mind, and I realised what I had done. My eyes brimming with tears, I stumbled to the gateway. Once outside, I fled into the darkness and sobbed uncontrollably.

Caiaphas

I have to say that I have had a most unsatisfactory day, though I would never admit it to anyone – least of all to my cantankerous old father-in-law, Annas. He would seize only too delightedly on any chink in my armour which might give him an opportunity of belittling me. I sometimes even suspect him of cooperating with the occupying power when it suits his devious purposes. I wouldn't put it past him to insinuate to the Roman procurator that I am not really up to the demands of the sensitive post of high priest of the Jews. And it certainly is a taxing appointment. I have to admit it takes all my skill, and too much of my time, to keep the peace between that wily politician Pilate and my next-to-impossible co-religionists.

Of course, I had seen today's crisis brewing for months. I seem to be forever doing a finely calculated balancing act with these would-be Messiahs. If I go along with them to any extent, I have the Sanhedrin in indignant uproar, quite often openly threatening to denounce me to the Romans as politically suspect. If I stamp on each one as soon as he appears, I am faced with an equally angry rabble, potentially even more dangerous if their unpredictable behaviour should attract the attention of the military. Today's case has turned out to be a classic example of my dilemma. Jesus of Nazareth has been hovering on the edge of national life – and therefore, of course, on mine – for some three years now, sometimes seeming to loom larger, at other times moving away from the centre of the stage. I initially decided to do what any urbane, civilised man such as myself would do: ignore him as much as I could but treat him with cool indifference whenever it proved impossible to ignore him. That excellent policy collapsed completely last Sunday when the man staged a provocative parody of a state entry into Jerusalem. In my opinion, he made a fool of himself by riding on a donkey, of all things, but he appeared to have judged his moment with masterly skill. Virtually the whole city went completely wild about him and invested his dramatic gesture with a religious significance which left us no choice but to regard both his action and himself as a challenge. For almost a whole day, we nearly lost control of the city, which would inevitably have meant a complete and final takeover by the Roman administration. To avert any further possibility of such a disaster, we were forced to consider ways of eliminating the man and the sooner the better, since Jerusalem was, of course, already rapidly filling up with Passover pilgrims – simple country folk, most of them, who would be easy prey for any mischief-maker intent on stirring up trouble at this always sensitive time of the year.

My problem then was simply to get Jesus out of the way. The challenge lay in how to achieve this without putting my own position and reputation at risk. Then fate played straight into my hands. For a surprisingly small sum, which I can only assume must have seemed like a fortune to a provincial peasant, one of Jesus's associates undertook to get him into our hands under cover of darkness, before the Passover festival. It all went without a hitch – although I had to allow myself a sardonic smile at the irony of having the very man I had determined to marginalise, right here, in my very own palace.

It was then that things began to unravel. I had naturally assumed that cursory compliance with the legal requirement for two witnesses to agree in their evidence against the accused would be a mere formality. Indeed, I had already taken the precaution of forewarning the procurator's staff that we would be making a request for a swift trial at first light this morning, with the clear implication that we expected an automatic clearance for execution – all in the interest of preserving public peace and order, you understand. I extricated myself from the unexpected difficulty with the prosecution witnesses by confronting Jesus directly with the question as to whether or not he claimed to be the Messiah, and when he broke his previous unsettling silence to say that he was, I felt a quiet satisfaction at having regained control of the situation. My backstairs contacts at the governor's palace did not let me down, and although that contemptible little man Pilate tried to derive some malicious pleasure at my expense by an unconvincing pretence at judging Jesus himself, our agents had no difficulty in manipulating the crowd. Pilate soon caved in, and, just as we had hoped, the execution began at nine o'clock this morning.

I had assumed that that would be the end of it all. But from noon until three o'clock it was, inexplicably and really rather frighteningly, dark here in the city. There have been unnerving earth tremors, and a short while back, a breathless and incoherent Temple guard rushed in and babbled something about the curtain in front of the holy of holies in the Temple having been torn in two from top to bottom. This is extremely alarming, but as if that were not enough to worry about, I am suffering from a ridiculously irrational but perversely persistent recollection of something I said in council a few weeks back now. With a touch more exasperation than I should have given into, I told the Sanhedrin, "You know nothing whatever; you do not use your judgement. It is more to your interest that one man should die for the people, than that the whole nation should be destroyed."

Why is that plaguing me so much today? Prophecy is dead, isn't it? And it has been for four hundred years or more now.

I have had a deeply disturbing day.

HEROD ANTIPAS

My dear, you can have simply no idea how wearisome it is to have to govern these uncouth Galilaeans. Neither my father's Idumaean ancestry nor my mother's Samaritan origins were of the slightest help in preparing me to cope with these implacably religious Jews. For over thirty years now, I have had to endure unrelenting flattery and treachery, hypocrisy and deceit, pretence and animosity such as I swear no ruler anywhere else in the whole of the Empire has had to contend with. What really galls me about it all is that I should never have had to suffer in this way at all. If my father's second will had been allowed to stand, I would now be king of Judaea or at the very least ethnarch. As it turned out, I was grievously wronged by the final disposition of my father's territories. I was unjustly reduced to being merely the tetrarch of Galilee and Peraea, while my older brother Archelaus was given Judaea. It helps not one whit to drone on about older sons taking precedence over younger ones, but it was indisputably my father's genuine intention that I should succeed him as king. To my dying day, I shall suspect Archelaus of having in some way blackmailed our father to alter his will – or perhaps of having it doctored after his death. I was reduced to the indignity of having to compete with that usurper for my lawful rights and then being subjected to the ignominy of seeing him installed where I should have been king while I was contemptuously fobbed off with only the northern and eastern regions of my rightful patrimony.

Pass the sherbet, will you, my dear? Thank you. I find it moderately refreshing in the heat of the day. Oh, and do have some yourself, won't you?

Now where was I? Oh yes, these turbulent Galilaeans. I've never liked them, and I gather the feeling is quite mutual. There was one in particular recently, to whom initially I took a strong dislike. He was one of those men from the wilderness of whom we seem to be having too many these days: a real religious crank – all shaggy hair and unkempt beard, with only a camel skin flung carelessly round him and a leather belt barely preserving his decency. Goodness only knows what he found to eat out in the desert. Herodias, the wife I took over from my half-brother Philip, sniggered when she first saw him, and she told him he looked as if he lived on locusts. I must say I was moderately impressed by his cool and steady gaze as he replied that that was exactly what he did live on – locusts and wild honey.

That first encounter between the two of them –my consort Herodias and John the Baptizer – gave me no hint whatsoever of the hideous dilemma the pair of them were to drive me into. It turned out that this wandering preacher had had the nerve to come to my capital city of Tiberias specifically to criticise me for having married Herodias. I don't mind admitting that I was torn between rage at the breathtaking insolence of this total nonentity and admiration for his quite extraordinary pluck in coming right into the heart of my court and delivering his completely uncalled-for comments with what certainly looked like utter fearlessness. Of course, I had no choice but to clap him in irons and incarcerate him in the dungeons beneath the palace. Then I found a strange thing happening. I began to feel uneasy and restless, but I discovered that these feelings disappeared completely every time I had John brought up from the cells and began talking with him and listening to him. There was an ethereal but very real aura of otherworldliness about him that I found utterly enthralling. I also felt that I was giving him a chance to make amends for his crassness in commenting publicly on my private life, but to my amazement he refused point-blank to shift his position. In anyone else I would have described it as a suicide-fixation, but I realised instinctively that with John it wasn't anything like that – he was immoveable because he simply knew that, on that particular issue at any rate, he was absolutely right. I daresay you would have called him a stubborn bigot, so would many others. I had, and still have, an unsettling suspicion that he was actually the very voice of God.

Inevitably, of course, Herodias got to hear about my discussions with John. She was predictably furious, and I suppose understandably so. She badgered me ceaselessly to have John executed, but I was developing quite a respect for the man, despite, or perhaps because of, his fearless criticism of my behaviour, and I kept postponing the order for his decapitation. But Herodias, as I have too often discovered to my cost, does not brook opposition.

Ah, there you are my dear; we were just talking about you. I was saying how cleverly you got me out of my dilemma over John the Baptizer. It was my birthday celebration, wasn't it? Didn't Salome dance enticingly? She was so ravishing that I got completely carried away, and as if in a dream, I heard myself promising her whatever she cared to ask for – even a half share in the government of the tetrarchy, if she wished (the wine had been flowing freely for some time by then, you understand). And you cleverly seized the opportunity to suggest that she ask for John's head on a plate, there and then.

I'll admit I was completely taken aback at first, but I quickly realised it was the perfect way of pleasing you, my dear, of preserving my credibility with all the guests who'd heard my brave promise to your daughter, and of getting rid of the thorn in your flesh without incurring direct responsibility for his death. He was certainly very popular with the lower classes, and I might have had a revolt on my hands if they'd been able to pin his death onto me.

But I'm talking too much. Where's that steward of mine? Chuza! Chuza! Have some more wine brought in.

Jerusalem at this time of year is stifling compared with the pleasant coolness of Tiberias. I have to come here for each of the main festivals, to keep my own people happy with what they think is my religious devotion and also to prevent my half-brother Philip from stealing a march on me by ingratiating himself with that loathsome Roman procurator, Pontius Pilate. But it is so deadly boring here; the only things to do are dull, respectable ones – or worse, religious ones.

Oh, what is it now, Chuza?

Really? A prisoner? Well, that may help to enliven an hour or two this morning. Sent from Pilate, eh? Should I smell a rat? Is he trying to trap me into doing or saying something which will justify him recommending to the emperor that I be deposed so that he can extend his own petty little authority? I must obviously go very carefully here. Oh no, do stay and watch the proceedings – they might even turn out to be entertaining.

Right. March in the prisoner.

Name?

Are you deaf, or something? I asked you your name.

Oh, give me the charge sheet, officer.

Jesus of Nazareth, eh? Well now, there's an unexpected stroke of luck. I've been trying to get to see you for quite some time. What is the charge against you?

Hmm, claiming to be a king. Well, it won't be the first time the royal house of Judaea has had to deal with impostors and would-be usurpers. My father took very strong measures indeed, some thirty or more years ago now, when he was told that a newborn baby was being set up as king of the Jews. I must say, you don't appear to have much idea as to how to go about it; you could at least make a more convincing effort to look the part.

What's that, officer? Is that so? I see.

My information is that you are the character who tried to disturb the peace of this city by staging some sort of demonstration here at the beginning of the week. That is indeed a serious charge. What have you to say to it?

Well?

I suppose it would be charitable of me to assume that you are completely overawed at standing in the presence of a prince of the Idumaean dynasty. I understand. I assure you that underneath my royal robes and golden crown, I am a very kind and reasonable person. Let's talk man to man. You do realise, don't you, that I have the power of life and death over you? You are one of my subjects. That is why Pilate has sent you to me. When I send you back to him, it will be with my recommendation either that you be executed or that you be released. Now, which would you prefer? Have you ever seen a crucifixion? Yes, of course you have. It doesn't bear thinking about, does it? But you're the man who has some sort of reputation for being one of these so-called miracle workers, aren't you? Perform a few miracles for me and my friends here, and I will return you to the procurator with my recommendation for your release.

Well, go on, turn this water into wine.

No? Oh, I suppose you can't manage that. Then how about healing young Alexas's leg? He broke it exercising in the gymnasium a couple of days ago.

Well, we are waiting.

Oh dear, is that beyond you too? We'll have to think of something easier, won't we? How about doing yourself a favour and snapping off those handcuffs you've got on?

Well, well, well. You are a disappointment to me. And to think that I was once afraid that you were my old enemy John the Baptizer come back to life after I had had him beheaded. What shall I do with you? I'll tell you what, Jesus, if you won't perform a miracle for me, I'll perform one for you. I'll make you look like the king you so pathetically claim to be. Chuza, fetch one of my old robes – the red one with the cloth-of-gold edging should do nicely. That's the one. Fasten the clasp at his throat. Oh my, doesn't he look right royal? Can we find a spare laurel wreath for his head? Oh, well done. No, straighten it up a bit. We can't have our would-be king looking drunk, can we? Here, stick this cane in his hand. I do declare, I haven't been so entertained for ages.

Do with him now? What d'you mean, *Do with him?* Send him straight back to Pilate, of course. No, no recommendation either way. The man and his fate are of supreme indifference to me.

PONTIUS PILATE

To Tiberius Caesar, Son of the god Augustus, Emperor
From Pontius Pilate, Procurator of the Province of Judaea

Greetings

I have thought it only right, Your Imperial Majesty, to acquaint you in some detail with the events which have unfolded in this province of Judaea since the date of my last written report to you. But first I express my sincere good wishes, and those of my wife, for Your Majesty's good health and perfect happiness, and I assure you of our unflinching loyalty to Your Majesty's person and our devout hopes and prayers for the complete success of all your interests and endeavours.

The people of Judaea repeatedly express their unqualified gratitude for the peace and prosperity they enjoy as a direct result of Your Majesty's beneficent rule. They count themselves fortunate indeed to be part of the great empire of the Romans. They are especially grateful for Your gracious and tolerant attitude to their religious beliefs and practices. For my part, however, I believe I should be failing in my duty to Your Majesty if I were not to comment that certain dangers may lurk beneath the surface of this enlightened policy.

You will already know that of all the peoples throughout Your vast dominions, the Jews are the most sensitive and intractable in the matter of religion. You will recall that they made an altogether disproportionate fuss when I ordered standards bearing representations of Your Imperial Person to be taken into the city of Jerusalem. As You also know, my attempt to placate them by replacing the standards with shields bearing only Your Majesty's name was most ungratefully seized upon as a pretext for continuing and wholly unjustifiable civil unrest. Nevertheless, in a magnanimous demonstration of our goodwill towards these difficult people, I authorised the construction of an aqueduct to bring much-needed water supplies into Jerusalem from the uplands south of the city. Since it will be the Jewish people who will benefit from this imaginative initiative, I naturally utilised for this purpose monies which their religious leaders had accumulated in the treasury of their Temple.

This entirely reasonable procedure was cynically exploited by disaffected elements, which I regret to say appear to have infiltrated the hitherto compliant Jewish leadership. I am happy to report that of course our troops had no difficulty at all in dealing with the ensuing little local disturbance; but I thought it prudent to make some sort of gesture which would leave nobody in any doubt as to who is in control, both of the city of Jerusalem and the province of Judaea. I therefore ordered the summary arrest and immediate execution of a number of Galilaeans attending one of the religious ceremonies at their Temple, and the aspersion of their blood on the sacrifices being offered at that time on the Temple altars.

My reason for making an example of Galilaeans on this occasion was that it would have the desired effect of stamping our authority unmistakably on these recalcitrant people without causing further trouble as a result since there are no particularly strong bonds between the Judaeans in the south of the country and the Galilaeans in the north. There has, however, been an unexpected development, which is the immediate reason for my writing to Your Majesty at this time. It seems that a populist leader from Nazareth in Galilee tried to capitalise on pretended Galilaean discontents by leading some sort of insurrectionist movement which, had I not nipped it in the bud, might have developed into an attempted uprising against Your Majesty's imperial power.

This movement was distinguished by its political overtones from the usual Jewish party activities, which are invariably religious in their emphases. Its leader, one Jesus, made a half-hearted attempt to disguise his own ambitions by using the phrase "the kingdom of God" in his appeals to his fellow countrymen, but this was clearly only a code to present himself to his hearers as a claimant to the throne of Judaea in open rebellion against Your Imperial Majesty.

I was not at first unduly alarmed by his activities; my men reported that when he was once asked whether it is lawful to pay the taxes levied by our administration, he requested the loan of a coin, and asked whose image and title it bore. When the answer was made "Caesar's", he apparently advised his hearers to give to Caesar what was Caesar's. My men therefore drifted away from the edge of the crowd, reasonably satisfied that he posed no serious threat to our power.

In the past week, however, this Jesus appears to have changed his tactics. I have made it my practice since taking up my appointment, to come to Jerusalem from my official residence at Caesarea for the duration of each of the main Jewish religious festivals. It seems politic to make a show of Your Majesty's authority at a time of heightened national awareness, in order to discourage any hotheads in the mob who might be tempted to take advantage of the opportunity to stir up unrest. At the same time, I believe it has the effect of soothing the populace at large by suggesting a certain respect for their religious beliefs and practices. As soon as I arrived for this year's Passover festival, the commander of the troops stationed in the tower of Antonia advised me that on the first day of this week he had felt it wise to put his men on alert because Jesus staged a small-scale and outwardly low-key processional entry into the city. However, Jesus's action, though seemingly impromptu, must have been pre-planned. Crowds of people materialised as if from nowhere with suspicious spontaneity, and for much of the day there were well-orchestrated shouts of welcome to "him who comes as king" and to "the coming kingdom of our father David". This clearly indicates that Jesus claimed descent from the former Jewish royal house, and it is certain that he was testing the strength of support for a possible uprising in his favour against Your Imperial Majesty, with a view, presumably, to taking the throne for himself in the unlikely event of his being successful. But with a peasant's predictable lack of even the most elementary political awareness, he promptly forfeited any chance of success by lashing out against the traders and stallholders in the Temple precinct who make a living out of meeting worshippers' ritual requirements.

This amusingly inept action on his part inevitably brought him into head-on collision with the religious leaders who could have provided him with his strongest support. My spies inform me that the Jewish establishment decided to remove the man from the scene before he caused them any further embarrassment, so I was not too surprised to receive a request for a trial on a capital charge. I was, however, taken aback when a priest-ridden rabble surged up to the gates of the residency first thing yesterday morning, and I was more than a little irritated by the very obvious attempt to pressurise me into granting perfunctory permission for execution. I therefore decided to remind these occupied people of their proper place, and I accordingly undertook my own investigation of the charges against Jesus.

Despite my earlier impression of political motivation, it initially seemed that the underlying reason for the Jewish leaders' wish to have

Jesus eliminated stemmed from religious hostility – they accused him of claiming to be their Messiah, apparently some sort of long-awaited religious leader. I therefore put the responsibility of judging him back into their court, but they declared that they had already found him guilty as charged and were merely seeking my formal endorsement of their automatic death penalty. I again declined to debase Your Majesty's Imperial power by authorising its exercise at the whim and fancy of distant foreign subjects, especially as my own questioning of the man revealed nothing in him even remotely deserving of execution – until, that is, his accusers suddenly and dramatically upgraded the charges against him by declaring that he claimed to be king of the Jews.

This, of course, immediately put the whole matter into an altogether different light. I had the prisoner brought from the public courtyard into the judgement hall and questioned him closely on this much more serious accusation. I found him remarkably calm for a man in his desperate plight, but of the greatest significance was the fact that when I faced him with the direct question, "Are you a king?" he made a reply which by no stretch of the imagination could be interpreted as a denial. Indeed, in the ensuing brief conversation he specifically used such words as *king, kingly authority*, and *subjects* in reference to himself, but he insisted that all this was to be understood as *other-worldly* – whatever that may mean. While I was still examining him, a servant came in with a message from my wife, urging me to have nothing to do with what she described as *that innocent man*; she said she had had disturbing dreams about him the previous night.

I therefore decided to try another ploy by utilising the annual custom of releasing a prisoner from custody as a gesture of acknowledgement towards the religious nature of the festival the Jews were then celebrating. I had Jesus brought out again and offered him as this year's prisoner for release; but to my considerable surprise, a unanimous cry went up for Barabbas, a convicted murderer. The crowd was clearly being manipulated by agents of the Jewish leadership. Your Majesty will of course know that I am the last person in the world to yield to intimidatory tactics of this sort; I therefore reiterated my judgement that the man was not guilty, and I announced that I would have him flogged as a salutary lesson and then released.

At this point, my clemency was eclipsed by my unshakeable loyalty to Your Imperial Person. The prosecution insinuated that to release a man who did not deny that he claimed to be a king would be tantamount to colluding with treason. I am happy to be able to prove to Your Majesty that the trust You so graciously placed in me when You first appointed me as procurator of Judaea has once again been totally vindicated. I first called for water, and I washed my hands in full view of the crowd in order to exonerate myself, and through me, Your Majesty and the entire Imperial administration of any taint of responsibility for the prisoner's self-inflicted fate. I then gave orders for the release of Barabbas and the crucifixion of Jesus – subject, of course, to the preparatory scourging – along with two other convicted criminals. I derived considerable pleasure from my success in infuriating the sickeningly self-righteous religious leaders by describing Jesus on the charge board above his head as *King of the Jews*. To their indignant protest that it should have read *He claimed to be King of the Jews*, I smiled, and merely replied, "What I have written, I have written."

Apparently, it took the man six hours to die.

SIMON OF CYRENE

You know, I'm really proud of those two sons of mine – or perhaps it would be more appropriate to say grateful for them. They've grown up to be splendid young men, even though I say it myself. People are always telling me what a credit they are to my wife and me: they're both strong but gentle, quick-witted and considerate, sensitive and happy, and they're always joking and laughing and forever pulling each other's leg about something or other. Mind you, there are differences between them – they're far from being identical. Alexander, the elder, is the more outgoing of the two. He's of average height, broad-shouldered, and a very good athlete; he developed his physique in the gymnasium here in Cyrene, much to the disapproval of the very strict leaders of our synagogue. Rufus, his younger brother, is taller and slimmer, with dark curly hair. Of course, he wanted to go to the gymnasium too, and he soon showed a real flair for archery. With excellent eyesight and rock-steady hands, he seems to be able to hit the target spot-on at least ten times out of twelve at a distance of fifty cubits or more. But although their early enthusiasm for exercising naked saddened their mother and me, they both remained faithful to our religion. In fact, looking back, I think I can see now that their contact with the world outside our Jewish culture was actually part of God's preparation for them to respond to the impact of Jesus. Now that they've reached their early manhood, in some sort of way that I can't describe very well they seem to have had their eyes opened to a much wider understanding of God and His ways with human beings. All I know is that I can talk about it because it's happened to me as well.

I shall never forget the one and only time I saw Jesus. I had gone to Judaea on business and counted myself blessed indeed that I was there over the time of the Passover festival. As a good Jew of the dispersion, I was looking forward to going on pilgrimage to the Holy City for the first time as the highlight of my life. I set out on the day before the Passover Sabbath. Every detail of the day is still indelibly branded on my mind. I got up at sunrise, and straightaway knew that it was going to be a very hot day. The sun was already blazing down by the time I started to walk the short distance to Jerusalem from the village where I was lodging. Spring was at the peak of its beauty: every fruit tree was a riot of blossom, the last of the winter rains had produced the annual miracle of lush green grass and luxuriant flowers, birdsong was an uninhibited outburst of exuberant joy, the cloudless sky was the luminous blue it can only ever be at that time of year – and then there were the people. Men and women, boys and girls, were all streaming along the paths and trackways down to the floor of the valley and then up the steep approaches to the city gates. Every now and then I heard snatches of one or other of the Songs of Ascent, and the sound of pipes playing the accompaniments. There was an inescapable sense of excitement and expectancy in the air; it seemed as if everything was combining to create an overwhelming atmosphere of religious solemnity and festival celebration – a profoundly satisfying fusion of holy day and holiday. And when I caught my first glimpse of the magnificent Temple, I felt a surge of deep emotion. It was dazzling white in the brilliant morning sun, rising splendidly above the city clustered round it. I had a fleeting mental picture of a mother hen watching solicitously over the brood of chicks all round her.

At that moment, nothing could have been further from my mind than the thought that I would never reach my goal, never set foot inside the court of Israel, never experience the exaltation of being present at the celebration of Passover in the very Temple itself. After all those years and having travelled all those miles, it was not even a possibility that anything or anybody would even try, let alone succeed, in stopping me from achieving the lifelong ambition of every devout Jew. But just as I reached the floor of the valley, some sort of commotion broke out at the gate in the wall for which I was heading. Roman soldiers appeared to be trying to clear a way through the crowds thronging the approach to the gate for a procession intent on moving counter to the stream of people pressing to enter. My stomach lurched as I realised that wooden beams were being carried in the middle of the little knot of people struggling to make progress against the tide of humanity fighting to get into the city. Sick with horror, I froze to the spot. Surely, this most holy and beautiful day was not about to be defiled by a crucifixion? But there was no point even in formulating the question, let alone trying to avoid the answer to it. With much shouting and brandishing of drawn swords, the soldiers cleared a path, and the grisly little procession weaved its way uncertainly down to the very spot where I was still standing, immobilised with shock.

As well as the soldiers, there were the women who out of sheer pity traditionally accompany condemned criminals to the place of execution, do what they can to show sympathy, and where possible, mitigate suffering, but in all conscience, there is really nothing at all they can do. Yet their presence, and their weeping and wailing, seemed to me, as an onlooker, to represent a last shred of humanity in the midst of unrelenting cruelty deliberately inflicted on the utterly helpless – a last affirmation of the solidarity of the living with those about to die. I was surprised to see a sizeable number of religious leaders following the condemned men, but my surprise turned to revulsion as it slowly dawned on me that they were actually mocking and jeering at the prisoners. I was, and still am, utterly at a loss to comprehend how they could reconcile their attitudes and actions with the fine words of their professions of faith, so familiar to anyone even half-acquainted with the formal rituals of synagogue worship. It seemed, moreover, that their attention was all centred on one man, although there were three being led to their deaths. Each of them seemed to be at his last gasp already. Huge bloodstains seeping through their wretched clothing betrayed the fact that they had each suffered the unimaginable torture of the scourge. Now they were being forced to walk to the place of execution with their hands tied to a six-foot beam of wood laid across their already-flagellated shoulders. Each had a board hanging on a rope round his neck, bearing a brief summary of the crime for which he was suffering. I just had time to read one of them – it said, *Jesus of Nazareth, the king of the Jews* – when the man stumbled and fell to the ground.

It couldn't have happened at a worse moment for the centurion in charge. A spontaneous gasp of sympathy swept the onlookers, followed by some audible protests when he swore and kicked out at the man on the ground. I saw two soldiers pull Jesus to his feet; two others detached themselves from the escorting party, and before I realised what was happening, they moved to each side of me and without a word propelled me into the centre of the group.

"You," snarled the centurion, "take this and carry it behind the prisoner." Obviously, I had no choice in the matter. I shouldered the long, heavy cross-beam and involuntarily winced as I imagined what it must have been like to have been carrying it on savagely lacerated shoulders. Then I realised that Jesus was talking. In a voice weak with pain, he spoke to the women accompanying the execution squad.

"Daughters of Jerusalem," he said, "do not weep for me, but weep for yourselves and your children"; and he went on to prophesy that terrible sufferings would soon engulf them and their city. Then the centurion barked an order, the soldiers surrounding us all moved on, and we had no option but to move with them.

I cannot bring myself to write down all that I saw and heard in the course of the next six hours or so; but I stayed to the bitter end and saw and heard it all. Incredible though it may seem, my experience that day has become the most precious thing in my whole life. I have met a number of followers of Jesus over the years since then, and what we have talked about together has brought me to the astonishing realisation that on that Passover eve, I was actually present at the consummation of the old religion of Israel and its replacement by the new faith, which is for everyone, including my Gentile neighbours, friends, and business contacts, as well as true-born full-blood Jews like me. Here in Cyrene, we have received a copy of a circular letter explaining that the annual sacrifice of a ritually pure lamb to atone for sin has been superseded by the once-for-all sacrifice of that morally perfect man whom we now know is the Son of God himself. I can still hardly grasp that I was there when it all happened.

Only last week, we had a message from young Rufus, in Rome. He's a keen member of the church there, and he wrote to say that they had had a letter from Paul, that tireless travelling Christian leader. Rufus is really delighted that he is mentioned by name in the letter, and he wanted his mother to know that Paul still remembers the way she looked after him all those years ago when they first met.

I said they're super boys, didn't I?

THE CENTURION

Barracks are pitiless places. When news came through of my posting to Cilicia and Syria, there was much joyless laughter at my expense. "Cilicia and Syria!" my fellow officers spluttered into their goblets, "you'll have a great time there – provided you ever find out where it is, of course! Isn't it the home of those religious nutcases, the Jews? Still, you're superstitious yourself, aren't you, old man? You'll feel quite at home there." I grinned weakly, and tried to appear to be taking it all in good part. In fact, I was very much in two minds about the whole thing. Half of me regarded my new posting in the same way most of my comrades did – a decidedly double-edged promotion. Certainly I was gratified at being made up to a centurion, but to be allocated to a small and obscure province at the south-east corner of the Empire, about as far from Rome as it was possible to get, seemed more like a sentence of banishment than anything else. On the other hand, the barrack-room jibe about the Jews being very religious people struck a responsive chord in me. I've always been fascinated by the wonder of life, and the various teachings which have been put forward in honest attempts to account for its mysteries and problems, its joys and its sorrows, the puzzles of who we are and why we are here, and where we have come from and where we are going – if anywhere. So I was as much intrigued as dismayed by my destination for my first posting abroad. Lysias, my excellent personal servant, set about making all the necessary arrangements for our journey to the Levant with his usual quiet efficiency.

My first assignment was to a place called Capernaum, in the tetrarchy of Galilee and Peraea. By the standards of the parts of the Empire that I have already seen in the course of active service, both district and town are quite undistinguished, but both are redeemed by the sizeable stretch of fresh water known as the Lake of Galilee. We were stationed in the town largely to stiffen the authority of the weak local ruler, Herod Antipas, but my duties were very far from onerous, and I had ample time, and many opportunities, to become acquainted with the Jewish religion. The more I learnt, the more I was impressed. As with all the religions I've so far come across, there are outward observances and ritual requirements, but they are all of a uniformly higher tone than any I've come across before. It seems to me that there is real point and purpose behind each one of them. Of course, to be a true Jew you have to be born of full-blood Jewish parents. But out of consideration for interested Gentiles, the Jewish religious authorities recognise a category of people they describe as God-fearers, and I'm perfectly happy for all my fellow officers and the men serving under me, to know that I now describe myself as exactly that: a God-fearer, with a capital *G*. The Jews have a mighty respect for their Law, and I can understand why: it's a code of moral and religious behaviour which is of a higher standard than any I've heard of before. I asked the local teacher of religion (they call him a rabbi) whether he would give me a course of instruction in it, and to my fairly considerable surprise, he agreed. I was even more surprised when he actually declined to accept payment, but I quickly got the message when he began hinting, delicately but unmistakably, that money was needed for the rebuilding of their local meeting house or *synagogue*. I happily chipped in with my contribution, and I'm glad to say that there is now a fine building for worship in Capernaum, in a lovely setting quite close to the lake.

But no sooner had the synagogue been completed than I experienced a major personal crisis. Lysias complained one day of not feeling at all well. This was the very first time he'd ever said any such thing in all the years he'd been with me, and I have to admit I didn't have the faintest idea what to do. Sure, most of my acquaintances would not have been in the least bit concerned about not having a clue as to what to do in such a situation – slaves are expendable and cheap to replace. But Lysias had been my utterly loyal and completely trustworthy attendant from the day I first bought him, when he was a bright-eyed, good-looking strong young teenager. As far as I was concerned, he wasn't expendable – he was indispensable. So my alarm increased in step with his rapid deterioration, until, seeing my desperation, one of my sympathetic Jewish friends suggested asking Jesus, the local freelance teacher and healer, if he could help.

In the inscrutable goodness of God, the man was that very day walking back to Capernaum after a training session with his followers in the hills. Some of the elders of the synagogue took up my friend's idea and volunteered to speak to him on my behalf. Beside myself with anxiety, I seized gratefully on their offer – as local worthies, they would be much more likely than I to carry weight with Jesus. Also, their cooperation meant that I would be able to stay with Lysias, who by now was sinking fast. Indeed, no sooner had the elders left, than he lapsed into unconsciousness.

With a surge of panic, I suddenly realised that he could be dead before Jesus reached my house, especially with all the crowds of people round him who habitually slowed his progress to a crawl. Lysias's breathing was becoming shallower and more rapid, and though his face was now deathly white, sweat was pouring from his handsome brow. I left him for a brief whispered conversation with the anxious bystanders, but this time I didn't wait for kind offers of help – I issued a crisp command to the two youngest of my men to run for all they were worth to Jesus and implore him to do something there and then, without even coming to the house.

In the meantime, a deputation of well-intentioned but maddeningly correct visitors from the synagogue, took what seemed to be ages in conveying their formal good wishes for my servant's recovery. I had the greatest difficulty in concealing my impatience, but I managed to maintain at least the outward courtesies before excusing myself to return to Lysias's room. I never got there – Lysias himself came strolling into the courtyard, perfectly fit, and smiling happily, and he asked me what my wishes were for dinner that night.

Life, as I have more than once discovered, has a ghastly capacity for doubling back on you with what sometimes seem to be hideously inappropriate coincidences. About two years after Jesus had so wonderfully healed my servant, I got a posting south to the garrison in Jerusalem. I had been there for less than a fortnight, when early one Friday morning I received an order from a member of the procurator's staff to oversee an execution. It was to be rushed through with all possible speed in order to be over and done with by sunset, when the very important Passover festival would begin. I selected a detail of four men, and we marched to the procurator's palace, where we took charge of two convicted thieves. I set up the customary flogging – in its dreadful way, a small help to them, since in most cases it hastened death through sheer loss of blood. I gathered from the noise coming from the front of the palace that some sort of trial was still under way – indeed, it seemed that the procurator was having difficulty in preventing a riot from breaking out. Then some of the soldiers of the palace guard brought a prisoner into the backyard – and I had the worst experience of my life, either before or since. They were pulling and pushing him, kicking and punching him, roaring with brutal laughter, and shouting out, "Hail, King Jesus!" I simply could not believe the evidence of my eyes and ears. I came out in a cold sweat as the awful fact dawned on me that this was indeed the very man who had so marvellously healed my servant in Capernaum, nearly two years previously. My immediate reaction was one of thankfulness that we had never actually met face-to-face, so Jesus could not know that the man he had so wonderfully helped was now to be responsible for his execution.

"You alright, sir?" I realised that one of my men was looking at me curiously.

"Yes, of course I am," I snapped, and moved casually back into the shadow of the colonnade. Looking back on it all now, I realise that although I was supposed to be in charge, I was actually swept helplessly along by the gathering momentum of events. As if in a bad dream, I watched the palace guard go through a sickening mockery of Jesus's alleged kingship. One soldier put on thick leather gloves to protect his own hands while he fashioned a circlet out of thorn twigs, which he then rammed down on Jesus's head. Someone else ripped Jesus's clothes off him and contemptuously flung an old purple robe round his shoulders, and then, to shouts of derision, each man came up to him, bowed or knelt in front of him with a mocking jeer, and, as he got up, slapped him round the face as hard as he could. I made an excuse to go into the palace while Jesus was being flogged, but I could not shirk my obligation to oversee the actual execution. We made our way out of the city with some difficulty – people were swarming in to attend the Passover celebration at the Temple. I had to requisition a passer-by to carry Jesus's crosspiece when he collapsed on the ground.

I was completely riveted by everything Jesus said and did in those last hours of his life. Everything he said and did set him apart, not just from the two others crucified with him, but from every other person I have ever met or heard of. He refused the drugged drink traditionally offered to victims to alleviate at least a little of the appalling pain they were about to suffer. Even as my men were hammering six-inch nails through his wrists and feet, he actually prayed for them to be forgiven. He promised life in paradise to one of the two men crucified with him who, in his own last extremity, acknowledged Jesus's kingship. The sight of his mother in the crowd round the crosses moved him to commend her to the care of one of his friends. I had never seen or heard anything remotely like this in any of the crucifixions I'd been involved in before. In his calm control of himself, and his care and concern for other people, even in the utmost depths of his own anguish, he towered above everyone else caught up in that grisly spectacle. There was not the slightest hint about him of anything approaching hatred or bitterness, despite the fact that a disgraceful claque of quite high-ranking religious leaders was standing right in front of him, taunting him to prove his Messiahship by freeing himself from the cross.

Towards noon, the highly charged atmosphere, generated by the potentially explosive mix of terrorisation by the occupying power and the resulting sullen hatred of the occupied people, began to subside. With their bloodlust satisfied and their ugly appetite for cruelty sated, the crowd began to drift away as the midday heat intensified. There was a stifling stillness in the air, and slowly but surely the level of light steadily dropped until, to my utter bafflement, it became almost too dark to see anything at all. The screams of pain and shrieks of agony from the men on the other two crosses had gradually subsided as the morning wore on, and for three hours there were only occasional low moans and gasps of anguish to be heard. Then my own nervous tension made me jump like a startled rabbit when Jesus suddenly cried out, loudly and agonisingly slowly, "My God, my God, why have you forsaken me?" A few minutes later, in a low, weak voice, he whispered, "I am so thirsty." Totally unnerved by the eerie atmosphere, one of my men sprang up, soaked a sponge in a bowl of wine, and held it on his spear up to Jesus's lips. Then with one last excruciating effort, Jesus summoned up all that remained of his rapidly ebbing strength, and with astonishing power and conviction shouted, "It is finished!" I moved closer to him and just heard him whisper, "Father, into your hands I commend my spirit." His body sagged, and I knew that he was dead.

I stepped back, and my voice choking with emotion, I said out loud, "Truly, this man was God's son."

There was a movement at my side, and I looked down. Lysias was on his knees, gazing up at Jesus with tears streaming down his face. I noticed that the sun was shining again, and all around the music of birdsong was filling the air.

Just like Us
III. Round the Crown

A Temple Guard

Well, I don't mind telling you, I'll be only too jolly well glad when this tour of duty is over. I've only been on call since last Monday – we do a week at a time, you know – but I swear this has been the busiest seven days I can remember in all the time I've served as a Temple guard. We had to make four arrests in as many days at the beginning of the week – and you'd never credit the things I've seen and heard since then. If you've got a minute or two to spare, I'll tell you about them, if you like –it's too hot to do anything else at this time of day, isn't it? Here, let's sit down in the shade of these olive trees.

It all started ordinarily enough. I reported at the Temple guardhouse first thing on Monday morning as usual, and our commanding officer went through the regular routine of receiving reports from the outgoing lot, and giving us the standard pep talk – you know, to ginger us up. The only different thing, course, was that it was Passover week. He made a lot of the obvious fact that there would be many more people in the city than usual, most of them pilgrims determined to get within sight and sound of all the religious goings-on in the Temple.

"You'll have your work cut out this week, my lads, and no mistake," he said in that condescending way our superiors always use when they're talking to us. I snorted inwardly – I've probably done more Passover weeks on duty than he's had hot dinners this month, and I've never yet met any trouble we couldn't handle.

But I have to admit, it did seem a bit different this year. There was a sort of feeling in the air – know what I mean? – you could hardly help noticing it. Those accursed Roman troops – inferior Gentiles, polluting our Holy City – seemed decidedly jumpy. I put it down to the rumpus made by that man from Galilee the day before my unit moved from reserve to active service. Some people say it was just him and his northern friends trying to stir up trouble by challenging us southerners to accept him as king. It would account for the Romans being on full alert, but it didn't seem very tactful, to put it mildly, to have soldiers of a foreign occupying power swarming all over Jerusalem at one of the holiest times of the year.

Anyway, we had a taste of what was to come straightaway. We'd hardly had time to settle in the guardhouse before a detail of six of us was told off to make an arrest for murder. We found the man alright, and we took him in charge, but I must say, he seemed a decent enough sort of a bloke to me – quietly-spoken, with a kind of distant, wistful look in his eyes, and he made no trouble at all when we arrested him and marched him off to the high priest's gaol.

That was the Monday, right? Lo and behold, five of us were settling down on Tuesday afternoon to a harmless little game of dice, when the commanding officer stomped in with what seemed like a copycat assignment, but it turned out to be a whole lot different from the previous case. The accused let fly a whole volley of oaths when we pushed our way into his house, and we had a fair old tussle to restrain him and get him tied up before we could frog-march him back to headquarters. He was effing and blinding something chronic all the way – I swear I learnt some words from him I'd never heard before.

Now you're never going to believe this – I hardly could myself – but as I live and breathe, exactly the same thing happened on Wednesday. This time I knew the chap: it was old Abbas's son, Barabbas, and he'd been the ringleader in a riot which had broken out in Jerusalem against the Romans. Our elders apparently thought they'd better keep in the Romans' good books, so they had Barabbas arrested themselves and then handed him over to the occupying power – fat chance he'd have of a fair trial from them, I thought. But I was proved wrong in a very unexpected way, as you'll hear in a minute.

61

So, three arrests for murder in three days. I just don't know what this city is coming to; it never used to be like this. Anyhow, on Thursday, all three were hauled before the Roman governor. I think our leaders wanted to get all outstanding executions out of the way before Passover on Saturday, and all three were duly sentenced to be crucified. A terrible business – I'm jolly glad it's Roman troops that have to do that, and not us. I'm as tough as the next man, but I couldn't do that to another human being, not even for money.

Well, as you can imagine, after three days on the trot, I was half expecting a call-out on Thursday. I wasn't disappointed, but it didn't come until late in the evening. We were all yawning and stretching and thinking of bed, when the old man suddenly burst into the guardroom and barked at us to get onto the parade ground at the double. There was a great deal of rushing round and issuing of swords and spears and truncheons and torches, but nobody seemed to have any idea of what it was all about.

"What's up, Sarge?" I asked our non-commissioned officer; but he just shook his head, and then, nodding towards a corner of the yard, said, "It's something to do with him."

I could just make out a figure standing well back underneath the arches, and then as someone carried a torch past him, I thought I recognised him. When we were all fell in, he emerged from the darkness and walked in front of us as we trooped out of the yard, through the city gate, across the Kidron, and into the Garden of Gethsemane.

With all the fuss and commotion, you'd have thought we were heading for a pitched battle with a regular army of bandits or something. But all that happened was that the fellow leading us went up to a man standing under the trees, said something like, "Hallo, Master", and kissed him. The chaps at the head of our column moved swiftly to grab hold of the man, and we suddenly realised that there were other men lurking in the shadows; I couldn't say how many – a dozen or so, at least. One of them lunged forward. In the flicker of light from torches there was the sudden flash of a drawn sword and a scream from a man ahead of me – his ear had been sliced off.

The prisoner said, "Let me at least do this," and he bent down, picked up the ear, and replaced it – just like that. I rubbed my eyes in disbelief, but it didn't alter the fact that the bloke was completely healed. It was as if absolutely nothing had happened to him – except there was blood on his tunic.

It all got a bit confused after that. The prisoner, whose name was Jesus, had a brief exchange with the officer, but we were keeping our eyes on the men behind him. To our surprise, they made no further attempts at resistance. They must have realised they were hopelessly outnumbered; there were certainly far more of us than were needed for this very minor assignment. Then their nerve suddenly broke, and they all turned and ran. I charged after one of them – he was in his late teens, with no clothes on at all and only clutching a scanty piece of cloth in front of him. I managed to grab hold of the cloth, but of course he just let go of it and fled into the night stark naked. I didn't bother to chase after him – he had a superb physique, and with youth and agility on his side, I knew I would never catch him.

Next day, back at the barracks, a rumour went round that Jesus, the man we'd arrested the previous night, had been found guilty of blasphemy by the Sanhedrin and had been taken before the Roman governor for confirmation of the death penalty. Apparently, Pilate wasn't convinced that he deserved to die and tried hard to get agreement that he should be freed. He offered him as the prisoner for release this year to mark the Passover festival, but the religious authorities incited the mob to shout for Barabbas, the very man we'd arrested only two days previously – so that was Wednesday's work wasted. Three men were crucified on Friday morning, as we expected, except that one of them was Jesus, instead of Barabbas. I wonder how Barabbas feels about that?

But the strangest thing of all was that that wasn't the end of my involvement with Jesus. Late on Friday afternoon, I was called out on a much more unusual assignment. Four of us were detailed to stand guard over a newly occupied tomb, but although the tomb belonged to Joseph of Arimathaea, he wasn't inside it – he was still alive and well. He'd made it available to Jesus's relatives and friends, in order to save his body from being thrown on the rubbish dump outside the city wall. But our religious masters had remembered something Jesus had said about returning to life three days after he died. They seemed to think his followers would try to spirit the body away, in order to be able to claim that his prophecy had come true. So, of course, we were under strict orders to see that nothing of the sort happened.

I thought it was going to be one of the quietest duties I'd ever had, and with nothing else to do, I fell to thinking. It seems very rum, doesn't it? When they took Jesus to Pilate, the charge that sealed his fate was that he claimed to be a king. Everyone seemed hell-bent on making a mockery of the claim. Apparently, the troops in the Roman barracks had stripped him of his clothes, flung an old purple robe round his shoulders, rammed a wreath made out of thorns down onto his forehead, stuck a cane in his right hand, and then bowed or knelt in front of him with drunken shouts of "Hail, King Jesus!"- before punching him in the face as hard as they could. But no sooner is he well and truly dead, than everyone goes out of their way to treat him as if he really were a king. Instead of being left to rot on the tip, like every other executed criminal, he was reverently wrapped in a proper winding sheet, solemnly carried to a private garden, and there gently laid in a brand-new tomb, never used for anyone else before. Then the establishment acknowledged his importance by sealing the tomb with official government –stamped seals, and my mates and I found ourselves on duty as a full-time formal guard of honour. It seemed that the authorities' actions revealed a great deal more about Jesus than anything they actually said about him.

I can't remember clearly what happened on Saturday night. I must have done the very thing I shouldn't have – fallen asleep on duty. Suddenly there was a searingly vivid flash of light, and the ground shook violently for a few seconds. Instinctively I drew my sword, though I don't know why. Then I swear my heart missed more than just one beat – the whacking great stone which had blocked the entrance to the tomb had rolled right to one side. Sweating with fear, we crept up and looked inside. Even in the predawn gloom, we could see there was nothing there – only an empty winding sheet. We agreed there was nothing we could do but report the facts. I can tell you, my professional pride really bristled at being ordered to say that Jesus's followers stole the body while we were asleep – the very thing we'd been stationed there to prevent. But I must say the money's come in very handy.

MARY OF MAGDALA

We saw him die. We *saw* him <u>die</u>. Surely few other women can have been subjected to so much passive suffering as the four of us who saw Jesus die – his mother, his aunt, my namesake (Cleopas's wife), and me. Can it perhaps even be true that we, of the so-called weaker sex, have greater reserves of strength, or possibly strength of a different kind, than men have?

Certainly I sensed the subtle change in the atmosphere here in Jerusalem very soon after Jesus made his dramatic appeal to the city – it doesn't seem possible that it is still only a week since it happened. The heady excitement of his lowly triumph on that day seemed to evaporate very rapidly, to be replaced by a feeling of relentlessly tightening tension and a sense of ominous foreboding. Try as I might, I just could not shake off a growing apprehensiveness for Jesus's safety. And when in the middle of Thursday night shaken and shocked disciples began trickling back to Mark's mother's house where we women had stayed to help clear up after the Passover meal Jesus had shared with them there, my worst fears were confirmed. But the possibility of debating what to do next was never even a remote consideration – the four of us did not even need to speak to each other. With that instinctive mutual understanding, which may be women's sixth sense, we set out at first light on the eve of the Passover for the palace of Caiaphas, the high priest.

There we learnt that Jesus had already been declared deserving of death and had been arraigned before the Roman governor. The governor was still considering the case when we reached his residence, and when, despite all our most fervent prayers, Jesus was handed over for execution, we followed the crowd gawping to see a crucifixion in a state of numbed shock. We kept well to the back, as much out of consideration for his mother as from fear of being recognised as his friends, but there was no escaping the impact of the hideous torture he endured, especially as the crowd thinned out towards midday. John was an absolute tower of strength; the only one of the men to show up at all when Jesus needed them most. He shepherded us women to the best of his ability and put his arm round Mary's shoulders when Jesus, knowing that death was imminent, asked him to care for her as if she were his own mother.

We tried to persuade Mary to leave the scene before the end, but drawing on her own inner reserves, she insisted that she would not desert him while the life she had given him still lingered within him. In a quiet, calm voice, she told us how clearly she remembered a prophecy which had been made to her when Jesus was only eight days old. When she and her husband took the baby to the Temple for his naming ceremony, an old man had said some mysterious but wonderful things about Jesus, and then, turning to her, he had said, "You will be pierced to the heart."

"I have had to live with that for thirty-three years," she said; "now I know what he meant."

So it was that we saw him die. When one of the soldiers casually flipped his spear into Jesus's side, I could not repress an involuntary cry of horror. But there was no response from Jesus – only a momentary gush of blood and what looked like a watery fluid, which quickly subsided to a slow trickle. My immediate reaction was actually one of relief; I suppose there must be a limit to what human beings can take in the way of suffering, and the realisation that he had finally moved beyond his unspeakable physical and spiritual agony enabled me to let go of the tension of my own mental and emotional anguish. It was replaced by a numbness, a deadness of any kind of feeling. I now realise that it was God's gracious way of enabling me to cope with the initial shock of the irreparable loss I had suffered. Emotionless, as if in a trance, we watched as Joseph of Arimathaea's men gently took Jesus's body down from the cross and wrapped it in a shroud. There was no time to embalm it properly – by now it was barely an hour to the start of the Sabbath. So we followed them the short distance to Joseph's garden and saw them lay him in the new tomb Joseph had only just had dug out of the rock for himself. It took five of them to roll the enormous stone along its groove to block the entrance to the tomb completely.

We spent the Passover in Mark's mother's house to avoid drawing any attention to ourselves. Already a heavy, dull ache was replacing the total absence of any kind of feeling which I had experienced on the Friday evening. A deep-seated need to do something to acknowledge and express our grief drove us to go out to the shops in the twilight after the end of the Sabbath to buy the spices for embalming the dead. A third night of uneasy, broken sleep ensued, but as soon as the first light of dawn broke the blackness on the eastern horizon, we crept silently out of the house, and with our cloaks wrapped round us against the early morning chill, we slipped quickly through the deserted city streets to Joseph's garden. We only stopped once, when I suddenly thought of the huge stone across the entrance to the tomb, but driven by our deep emotional need to be near to Jesus, and to do something, anything, however seemingly pointless, for him, we hurried on again.

When we reached the garden, the stone was back where it had started, and the tomb was open. We all stood stock-still. I remember that my first reaction was that I was dreaming, but the sound of a cockerel crowing jerked me back to reality. Then I thought that the early morning mist and the grey light of dawn must be playing tricks with my eyes, but the light was brightening with every minute, and I realised that I simply could not doubt the indisputable evidence of my senses. With all my faculties now shocked into total alertness, I noticed the first stirring of the breeze lightly rippling the top of the grass. Shivering now more from apprehension than cold, we clutched each other for support and moved slowly to the entrance.

We were greeted with the most dazzling smiles I have ever seen, or am ever likely to see, from two startlingly good-looking young men sitting where we had seen Jesus's body laid, but the body was not there – only the shroud in which it had been wrapped, with bloodstains showing where it had touched his hands and feet and side. In a most marvellously gentle voice, one of the two said, "Do not be alarmed. You are looking for Jesus of Nazareth, who was crucified. He has been raised; he is not here. Look, there is where they laid him. But go and tell his disciples and Peter that he is going ahead of you to Galilee; you will see him there, just as he told you."

Stupefied with incomprehension, none of us was able to say a word. We just looked at each other open-mouthed and then turned and fled, without even so much as a backward look. Oblivious now to what anyone might think or say, we ran and gasped and stumbled and panted through the slowly awakening streets back to Mark's mother's house.

Looking back on it now, I can understand the men's reaction. Inevitably, they dismissed our disjointed babbling as merely the expression of grief-induced hallucination. But as we slowly began to calm down, I suddenly remembered the young man's specific mention of Peter. He sat bolt upright when I told him, and then he slowly rose and made for the door. His move caught John's eye, and he went out with him. There was a noticeable change in them both when they returned some time later. Peter was now sombre, where he had previously been sunk in inconsolable despair, and John's aura of unfathomable private loss appeared to have given way to a deep sense of peace, which slowly but surely began to communicate itself to the rest of us. As soon as he came through the door at the top of the stairs, he came over to me, bent down, and whispered, "I believe it's true – he really has returned to life."

My mind in a total whirl, I left the upper room and retraced my steps to Joseph's garden. The daily life of the city was now in full swing, and all the usual sights and scents and sounds of people about their everyday business helped to restore some semblance of balance to my thoughts and feelings. But I experienced another unsettling shock when I saw that the entrance to the tomb was still open, and that the stone was still firmly back in its original position. Suddenly, the accumulated pressure of all the stress and tension of the previous week proved too much for me, and I was swept by a storm of uncontrollable sobbing. Driven by an overwhelming need to be with Jesus again, I stumbled to the entrance. The two handsome youths were still there, and one of them gently asked me why I was crying. I blurted out that Jesus had been taken away, and I didn't know where he was, and then, embarrassed by my own weeping, I turned away. In the bright sunlight, contrasting so strongly with the cool, dark interior of the tomb, I saw a man standing whom I assumed to be Joseph's gardener. Still half blinded by my tears, I begged him to tell me where he had put Jesus's body. He spoke one word: my name, "Mary."

That split second is indelibly burnt, not only into my memory, not just into my heart, not even merely into my mind, but into my whole life and being. The very world held its breath, and free from any pressure of time, I was able to listen to the songs of the birds, to absorb the scents of the flowers, and to notice the waving of the palm branches caressed by the wind. Then, from the depths of an utterly new, inalienable tranquillity, I acknowledged him: "My master!"

Now nothing else in heaven or on earth has any place in my life. I think day and night of the little story I once heard him tell, of the evil spirit who was expelled from someone's life and, after wandering about looking fruitlessly for someone else to go to, chanced again upon the life he had been driven from and found it clean and healthy, sweet and fresh. Jesus had gone on to warn that if a new and good master was not invited in, the dispossessed demon would return with six other spirits worse than himself. I had already reached that state when I first met Jesus. He freed me from not one, but seven, devils. Is it any wonder, then, that I have anointed him – who lived and died and now lives again, and lives for evermore – as king of my whole being?

JOHN

When I stop to think about it, I realise that I have always related well with men older than I am. I suppose it's because I'm the younger brother. I always looked up to James when we were boys, and although he treated me as an equal, it just seemed natural that he always took the decisions, made the choices, and told me what to do. I was very intrigued when I twice heard Jesus tell stories about two sons and their relationships with their fathers – had he got Dad, James, and me at the back of his mind? Or perhaps our best mates Simon and Andrew and their father, old Barjonah? Maybe not, but what is certain is that I took to Jesus from the very first time I ever met him. There was an instant rapport between us, which we both recognised and which has strengthened and developed ever since. Only men who have themselves experienced this kind of bonding will understand what I am talking about.

The fact that we had been shaped by different environments had no effect at all on our relationship. Jesus came from the hills and was a carpenter by trade; whereas I'm a fisherman, and up until the time I met him, I'd spent almost my entire life on and beside the lake. In fact, my first meeting with him took place beside the water, but it was the water of the river Jordan, not of the lake of Galilee. At home in Capernaum, we'd heard talk about a wandering preacher down south with the same name as mine who was causing quite a stir with his fearless comments about tax-collectors, soldiers, and even, apparently, religious leaders. Andrew, Simon, and I decided we'd like to hear this John for ourselves. By all accounts, he seemed to be cast in the mould of one of the great prophets of old, and we hadn't had one of them for a good four hundred years or more. Dad reckoned he and James could keep the business ticking over satisfactorily with the help of the hired men for a few weeks or so, so we set off for the south.

We had no trouble in tracking John down – the whole of the Jordan valley was fairly buzzing with gossip about him. Yet the odd thing was that no sooner had we located him and begun to get to know him a bit, than he seemed to want to get rid of us – or, more accurately, to pass us on to someone else. He'd been insisting that he was only a messenger, a herald, a sort of signpost – and then suddenly, one afternoon he pointed to a man walking along the river bank and said, "That's him – that's the one I've been sent to announce."

Out of curiosity, Andrew and I got up and went after him – and that's how I first met Jesus. We talked for hours, and I felt an overwhelming sense of having arrived, of being at home, of belonging, of security, of fulfilment, and of deep, deep peace.

That meant a lot to me, because out on the lake, back at the job again, I was often away from home all night, and as insecure as only a man can be who has been caught in one of those furious squalls for which Galilee is famous – or perhaps I should say infamous. And as for the feeling of having arrived – there was one never-to-be-forgotten occasion when, I must say against my better instincts, we set off at dusk from the eastern shore to sail the seven miles or so back to Capernaum on the western side. Now that's no great distance in anyone's book, and I'd done it many times before. But the storm that brewed that night was just about the most ferocious I can recall, either before or since. Our single sail was no use at all – the northerly gale ripped it to shreds in no time at all as we tried endlessly to tack across the wind, and we were soon reduced to struggling fruitlessly with the oars. Although everyone tried his best to help, by no means were all twelve of us sailors – Matthew spent almost the entire trip leaning over the stern being sick – and against the screaming wind and the mountainous waves we were making no progress at all. I really was getting to feel worried about our chances of survival. By my reckoning, we'd been a good six hours or more battling against the storm, and although we'd long since lost sight of the eastern shore, there was not a glimmer of light anywhere to indicate the position of the western shore.

But then, ceaselessly straining to see through the rain-lashed darkness, I suddenly thought I saw a faint light astern on the water. At first, I wondered if it was a lantern on another boat, although we certainly hadn't seen anything else on the lake from the moment we set sail. Unbelievably, given the conditions, the light seemed to be steadily catching up with us, until it slowly dawned on me that it was in the shape of a human figure. Presumably, the others were stretched to breaking point by the stress of the night's experiences – they all started shrieking absurdly about ghosts and the like. But as I gazed intently at the figure, I suddenly realised that it was Jesus, and I said as much to Simon. Impetuous as ever, he swung over the side of the boat and

actually began to walk across the water to Jesus. Of course, we helped
them both on board. In our highly charged emotional state, we never
noticed that the wind had died right down and the waves had subsided
to a gentle swell, until suddenly, only a few hundred yards away in the
first light of a new day, we saw the familiar hills around Capernaum,
serenely unmoved by the fury of the storm which had battered us all
night.

Reflecting on all this later, I slowly began to grasp that, amongst
other things, we were being prepared for the much more terrible storm
that finally broke over us just a month ago now. I remember being
frightened more than once when Jesus started talking about death –
his own death – and completely mystified when he went on to speak
about returning to life three days later. But now it has all happened. An
ominous atmosphere of mounting threat and nameless danger clouded
the week leading up to Passover, until it completely swamped us on the
Thursday evening. We knew ourselves then to be as helpless against
events as we had been against the elements on the lake. Although I
had two advantages over the others – my acquaintance with a member
of the High Priest's staff, which enabled me to obtain admission to
the courtyard of the palace when Jesus was taken there for trial by the
religious authorities, and my youth, which helped me to steel myself
to follow him to Golgotha when he was taken there for execution by
the political power – I watched him endure the unspeakable horrors
of death by crucifixion. I knew then that the bond between us was
unbreakable. And for pure love of him, I gladly responded to his last
request to me – to take his mother into my family as my own mother. I
am both humbled and elated that he committed her to me in preference
to anyone else.

And then came Sunday morning and the first day of a new week.
For me, it felt like the end of everything. Half of me – more than half
of me – had died with Jesus, and now that he was buried, hope and love
and life itself all seemed to be buried with him. My numb desolation
was not in the least bit helped by the hysterical babbling of Mary of
Magdala when she got back from an early morning visit to Jesus's tomb.
Yet when she kept on insisting that his body had gone, Simon caught
my eye, and with never a word spoken between us, we went out and
headed for Joseph of Arimathaea's garden. We walked at first, but an
urgent need to know what had happened impelled me to quicken my

pace until, in no time at all, I had broken into a run and left Simon to lumber along on his own as best he could.

So when I reached the garden, I was entirely alone; I shall always thank God that I was. The run had increased my heartbeat, but when I saw the entrance to the tomb open, it stopped completely for a split second and then surged again at a furious rate. Simon stumbled up, red-faced and panting, and with no hint of hesitation or decorum, blundered right into the tomb. I took a couple of deep breaths and moved slowly forward. Mary was right – absolutely right. The tomb was completely empty, apart, that is, from the winding sheet and headband, both lying flat on the slab. All I can say about that moment is that it totally remade me. The realisation flooded over me that he had not been removed from the tomb but had risen from death, and I knew immediately that his restored life meant that I too was a new man.

Simon was too breathless for words, and I was too awed to speak. We emerged blinking into the sunlight and slowly retraced our steps. The rest of the day is a confused blur in my mind of people coming and going; of repeated reports that now this one, now that one, had seen and heard Jesus for themselves; of the mood in the upper room swinging wildly between open-mouthed incredulity and rapturous excitement; but through it all, I was conscious of a peace even more profound than that I had experienced when I first met him, a stillness more intense than the calm of the lake in the tranquil light of sunrise after the storm which had threatened to take us all to the bottom.

And it was just such another dawn of unearthly beauty that that unpredictable lake gave us only a few days ago. I've spent countless nights out on the water, but I don't think I can remember another when we had caught absolutely nothing, not even a single solitary tiddler. But it was hardly surprising – my mind was still reeling from the impact of all the shocks of the past few weeks, and my heart simply wasn't in my work. The lake was totally calm; not a ripple broke the surface of the water, and as the darkness over the eastern hills slowly lightened and lifted, I abandoned the futile struggle, stripped completely, and sat in the prow of the boat, gazing dreamily across the utter stillness of the water. Thin, early morning mist was drifting lazily along the water's edge. After a while, I thought I saw smoke as well as mist on the shore. At first, I wondered if my eyes were playing tricks on me, but as I concentrated my gaze, I saw a tiny flicker of flame. I sat bolt upright, and at that instant the unmistakable voice of Jesus came clear across the motionless water, asking if we'd caught anything.

"Try trawling on the other side of the boat," he said.

"It's the Lord!" I gasped.

Simon, as naked as I was, flung the net in again and was immediately pulled overboard by the weight of the fish caught in it. He leant back into the boat, grabbed his loin-cloth, and waded to the shore, leaving us to cope with the heaving harvest of the lake, threshing and splashing and bidding fair to split our net wide open.

The experience of the next two hours or so is almost impossible to describe. Even the grounding of the boat on the pebbles seemed like a blasphemous intrusion on the serenity of the scene. I noticed how carefully all six of us climbed out of the boat and paddled quietly ashore. The intensity of the experience is still as vivid as it was then; the absolute peace that prevailed penetrated to depths of being I had not plumbed before. There was not a soul in sight to distract us from Jesus, not a sound to disturb the silent ecstasy of seeing him again, of listening to him anew, of gratefully sharing breakfast with him as we had done nearly every day for the whole of the previous three years. I sat on the edge of the group, but in the perfect atmosphere of that marvellous mystical morning, I heard every word of the infinitely gentle but deeply moving reconciliation between Simon and Jesus. No matter how little or how long I still have to live, I know that no other experience whatsoever will ever be able to match the distilled exaltation of that first communion with my living Lord.

CLEOPAS'S FRIEND

Come on, young Cleopas, get your lazy head off that pallet – you should have been up hours ago. It's a beautiful day, just perfect for a seven-mile walk. Goodness knows, you should be in fine form for it, what with two practices in less than forty-eight hours.

Ah, there you are. Well, I must say, that cheerful grin couldn't be further from the unrelieved gloom on your face when we did this walk on Sunday. But I know exactly how you're feeling, lad – I'm that way myself, only more so. I can still hardly believe it's all true, can you? Still, you can't contradict the evidence of your senses, is what I say. I swear I'm still experiencing the aftershock of seeing the nail wounds in his wrists when he took the bread on our supper table and broke it into three; they were so obviously recently inflicted – they'd barely stopped bleeding, it seemed to me.

Sorry, what were you saying? I can't keep up with you, what with all these people crowding the street. It'll be better once we're outside the city gate. Oh yes, that's right. That's very true, Cleopas. He didn't force himself on our senses, did he? Fancy us walking and talking all that way with him without realising it was him – not even recognising his voice! I suppose it's because he was the very last person we were expecting to meet that day – or any other day for that matter. I mean, nobody could have been more dead than he was after all he'd been through. D'you know, it's just beginning to dawn on me. Was he deliberately half hiding himself from us, sort of trying to reduce our dependence on the evidence of our senses, and somehow – oh, I don't know – to move us on to a higher stage, realising that he is still living and working with us, but accepting that fact by faith, rather than by merely seeing him and hearing him with our physical senses? What do you think, Cleopas?

Ah, that's better. I can keep up with you now. It was just a little farther along this stretch that Jesus caught up with us on Sunday afternoon, wasn't it – exactly where the path turns right to skirt old Jonas's vineyard? I shall never forget it, will you? How on earth could we fail to recognise him? But didn't he deal gently with us? I shall always remember how politely he asked what it was that was making us so miserable. Your face was a perfect give-away, Cleopas – did you know that? You just stood stock-still in disbelief and more or less accused him of being the only person in the whole of Jerusalem who didn't know what had been going on there last week. And then his simple question – "What things?" – just seemed to unblock all our pent-up emotions: bereavement, bewilderment, and fear. Between us, we unleashed a torrent of words at him, didn't we – explaining, complaining, grieving, questioning? How patiently he listened. He obviously knew immediately that we needed to release all the strains and pressures that had built up inside us since the excitement of his dramatic entry into the city a week ago last Sunday.

And then he started the healing process, didn't he? His very voice was a soothing balm as we resumed our walk, wasn't it? You and I both fell completely silent as he gave us such teaching as we've never heard before, from scribe or rabbi, in synagogue or Temple. Mind that overhanging branch there; you were so engrossed in what you were hearing last Sunday, that you walked right into it. Don't you remember?

Oh yes, I agree completely. I'll never be able to puzzle out why he chose to spend more than two hours with just the pair of us last Sunday afternoon; but it makes it all the more imperative that we're both absolutely sure of exactly what it was he told us so that we can pass it all on accurately to the others. You know, of all the Scriptures he explained to us, I think it's the passage from Isaiah that stands out most vividly in my mind. Goodness knows I've heard it read often enough – once I even read it out loud myself when I was handed that particular scroll one Sabbath in the synagogue back home. To be honest with you, I've never really known how to make head or tail of it before: but now – my word, it has positively leapt into life. What was such a puzzle has all fallen into place. Every phrase fits perfectly with what we have witnessed in the past week, doesn't it? There we were, all looking for a charismatic character, probably born in a palace, certainly born to command – young, good-looking, irresistibly attractive – and then Jesus pointed out that what Isaiah actually said was that God's chosen one would have no beauty or majesty to attract us to him, nothing striking in his appearance that we should desire him. Indeed, the opposite would be true –he would be despised and rejected by men; he would be a man of sorrows and familiar with suffering. But it wasn't until after Jesus left us at Emmaus that it suddenly dawned on me that those words described him exactly.

And all those bits I ignored because I couldn't understand them:

"He has borne our infirmities and carried our diseases:
He was wounded for our transgressions, crushed for our iniquities;
Upon him was the punishment that made us whole,
And by his bruises we are healed"

Now they all make perfect sense. We both believed he was the Messiah, didn't we, Cleopas? But we still expected a national military leader who would lead us to victorious war against the Romans and then set Israel up as ruler of the world. Instead, it was our world which simply fell apart at the end of last week, wasn't it? We were all completely shattered when he let himself be arrested without a fight, be tried without protest, and be executed without resistance. What kind of Messiah was that? And yet there it all was in the Scriptures, as clear as daylight for anyone to see:

"He was oppressed, and he was afflicted,
Yet he did not open his mouth;
Like a lamb that is led to the slaughter,
And like a sheep that before its shearers is silent,
So he did not open his mouth."

Now that Jesus has made the connection for us, I can't for the life of me understand how I didn't see it all beforehand:

"He was cut off from the land of the living,
Stricken for the transgression of my people.
They made his grave with the wicked
And his tomb with the rich,
Although he had done no violence,
And there was no deceit in his mouth."

Every word fits perfectly, doesn't it? And how long ago did Isaiah write his book – seven hundred years or more, wasn't it? Can you really take it in, Cleopas, that it has all been fulfilled in our own lifetime? I don't know about you, but I'm still reeling from the impact of all that's happened in the last few days. It's as if the whole world has turned completely upside down – or rather it's suddenly turned the right way up.

Say that again, Cleopas – I didn't quite catch you. Oh yes, and even more illuminating was the way he explained what all this suffering achieved:

> "All we like sheep have gone astray;
> We have all turned to our own way:
> And the Lord has laid on him the iniquity of us all.
> He bore the sin of many,
> And made intercession for the transgressors."

Now everything has been totally transformed, hasn't it? Now that we know that our fellow traveller on Sunday afternoon really was Jesus himself, alive again, the rest of Isaiah's words have become unmistakably clear, haven't they?

> "See, my servant shall prosper;
> He shall be exalted and lifted up, and shall be very high.
> He shall see his offspring, and shall prolong his days;
> Out of his anguish he shall see light.
> The righteous one, my servant, shall make many righteous."

What's that, Cleopas? Oh yes, I see what you mean. I suppose I have done most of the talking so far! Really? All of it?

Oh, surely not! Well, I'm very sorry, but I honestly can't help myself. It's as if I've come out of deepest darkness into most marvellous light. Don't you feel the same? Yes, I agree. It's even more than that; it's as if we ourselves have been lifted out of death and carried up into life. I honestly don't think I shall ever be able to stop talking about it – it really is world-shattering. Everything has been made new, and everyone must be told about it. What was it Isaiah said in the same passage?

> "Who has believed what we have heard?
> And to whom has the arm of the Lord been revealed?"

But he'd already answered his own question, hadn't he?

> "He shall startle many nations;
> Kings shall shut their mouths because of him:

For that which had not been told them they shall see,
And that which they had not heard they shall contemplate."

I guess we'd better start just as soon as we reach Emmaus, don't you, Cleopas?

NATHANAEL

Strange, isn't it, how life moves slowly along, day after day, week after week, month after month, in the same old routine, with nothing out of the ordinary happening – and then suddenly, without any warning at all, a single, solitary, perfectly normal event instantly turns everything upside down with ongoing consequences you would never have imagined possible, not even in your wildest dreams. I so well remember my old Dad once remarking that life is a matter of years of unwitting preparation for the moment of unexpected crisis. I remember it so well because that's been exactly my own experience. All that happened was that a friend of mine introduced me to a friend of his. There could hardly be anything less unusual than that, now could there? It must happen everywhere, every day, surely, it's one of the things that friends are for, isn't it? But let me begin at the beginning.

Philip and I have been friends all our lives. We both were born in Bethsaida, we both played together in the market square as youngsters, and we both were taught by the same rabbi in the synagogue school there. Later, I moved away to Cana to find work, but although that put a good twenty miles between us, we've always kept in touch with each other. We were together on that never-to-be-forgotten day which totally transformed life for both of us.

We'd heard rumours in Galilee about a character who'd apparently emerged from the desert and was drawing large crowds down south with his fiery preaching; people were even wondering whether he might be the eagerly awaited Messiah. Philip and I agreed that this sounded too exciting for us to leave to other people's reports, so we both took time off from work and set off to investigate for ourselves.

Now I'll cheerfully admit that I enjoy my food. I'm fortunate in being strong and healthy, and I eat well so as to stay that way. So the sight of a fig tree loaded with fruit on a hot afternoon in the Jordan valley proved irresistible to me. Philip said he wasn't hungry, so he went on while I enjoyed the delicious taste of ripe figs fresh from the tree. I'd actually sat down in the welcome shade of the tree and was blissfully drifting off to sleep when Philip suddenly pounded up, shook me roughly by the shoulder, and fairly shouted, "Wake up, Nathanael, wake up!"

"What on earth's the matter?" I demanded irritably.

His eyes shining with excitement, he blurted out, "We've found the Messiah!"

I stood up, stretched, and yawned. "Well, that's great news," I said, "that's exactly what we came here to do. So John has made a public announcement – or did you find him and ask him yourself?"

"No, no, it's not John at all – it's his cousin Jesus, son of Joseph, from Nazareth!"

Suddenly I was fully awake. "Nazareth? Nazareth?" I repeated incredulously. "Nothing good ever came from there! You've been out in the sun too long, Philip. It must have gone to your head; here, come and sit down in the shade and cool off a bit." I might as well have saved my breath – he was already pulling me along, and although I was initially annoyed at being hustled like that, his enthusiasm soon wore down my hostility.

"Where are we going?" I asked.

But all he would say was, "Come and see."

What I saw was a man of about my own age or a little older, perhaps just turned thirty, of medium height with long dark hair and the strong forearms of a worker clearly accustomed to wielding saw and plane, hammer and chisel. He was dressed in exactly the same way as the rest of us, with nothing about him to distinguish him from anyone else – apart, that is, from his expression. There was a smile playing round his lips but an intensity about the steady gaze of his eyes which instantly made me feel, however absurd it may sound, that he already knew me through and through. His first remark to me was a compliment far above anything required by conventional good manners.

"Here is truly an Israelite," he said, "in whom there is no deceit."

Startled, I asked, "How did you get to know me?"

"I saw you under the fig tree before Philip called you," he replied. From that day to this, I have never known what came over me, but I heard myself saying, "Rabbi, you are the Son of God! You are the King of Israel!"

All I know is that that was my own moment of crisis for which all the preceding years of my life had been the preparation, and nothing I've seen or heard since has ever given me the slightest reason to consider changing my mind about him.

David Gurney

By a most happy coincidence – that's serendipity for you! – I was able to start getting to know Jesus straightaway. He mentioned that he'd been invited to a wedding in Cana, my home town, so he and I made the return journey north together, along with Simon and his brother Andrew, and Philip and John. We learned a lot from what he said in those few days of leisurely walking – but nothing like what we learned in a few minutes at the wedding reception when we got to Cana. More people turned up than were expected, and our hosts were covered with shame and embarrassment when the wine ran out. But Jesus saved the situation with a minimum of fuss. He told the caterers to fill several large stone jars with water and then run some off for the best man to sample. We all were as surprised as he was at the excellent quality of what was the finest wine I could ever remember tasting, before or since.

I didn't go back to my job after that. Instead, with eleven others, I followed Jesus full-time, watching, listening, and learning as he preached, taught, and healed. We moved all round Galilee, sometimes south into Judaea, once or twice north of Galilee, and occasionally east into the desert. I was particularly impressed by Jesus's concern with the whole of human life. His preaching about the arrival of the kingdom of God was thoroughly spiritual. His teaching about what that meant in terms of attitudes and behaviour was intellectually challenging and mentally stretching. His healing demonstrated his interest in people's physical health and well-being. It wasn't just limited to those who were ill, either – more than once he took a mere snack and turned it into a satisfying meal for four or five thousand hungry people; and although we didn't necessarily see it that way at the time, we later realised that what he was really doing was dramatizing his message.

We couldn't always grasp what he was saying in words, but we could absorb what he was trying to get over by watching what he did and then thinking it through for ourselves afterwards. For instance, once in Jerusalem he described himself as water which would slake thirst eternally. He declared he was the true bread, from heaven, given to sustain life for evermore. Finally, at the last meal we had with him before he was arrested, tried, and executed, his passionate desire to convey God to us, and us to God, reached the ultimate height of self-denying intensity when he said that the bread and wine we were eating and drinking were his body and blood. Ever since then, the food and drink I still greatly enjoy for their own sake have taken on a new significance for me – I realise that they can, and do, represent the new relationship between him and me brought about by his death and resurrection.

But as far as I'm concerned, part of the good news is that he is still concerned with the whole person, body and mind, as well as spirit. I keep having to remind myself that it was physical death he conquered, and that it was his own previous physical body in which he came back to us when he was restored to life. Perhaps the most convincing thing he did for us in the large upper room of Mark's mother's house in Jerusalem, barely three days after he'd been crucified, was to ask for some cooked fish and calmly sit there and eat it in front of us all, just as he'd so often done in the three years or so we'd already spent with him. And it was the smell of fish being grilled over an open fire, drifting across my nostrils in the first light of sunrise one utterly still morning on lake Galilee a few weeks later, which alerted me to the fact that he'd prepared breakfast on the beach for the seven of us who'd been struggling for a catch all night without the slightest smidgen of success. That was an intensely moving experience – but I'm no good at describing such deep things; ask John if you want to know more about it.

One thing has always puzzled me though, and it concerns a fig tree again. One morning in his last week in Jerusalem, Jesus went up to a fig tree, hoping to find some fruit on it. When he didn't, he said, "May no fruit ever come from you again!" When we passed the same way again next morning, the tree had withered right up. I worried about this for quite a while, and eventually I plucked up courage to talk it over with Matthew. He said he thought it might be a prophecy of judgement to come on our people for having rejected Jesus – a sort of acted parable, as it were. I wonder if he's right? I tremble when I think that he might be.

Thomas

Being a twin can have its downside as well as its advantages. I never knew my twin brother – he died very soon after we were born. But I've known all my life that something has been missing, something fundamental to my very being. I'm always conscious of a hole in my existence – it's as if I have to cope with everything with one hand tied behind my back. As a result, I feel insecure and unsure of myself. I always seem to need reassurance from other people. Mind you, I don't want to give the impression that I'm permanently moody and miserable; for the last three years I've found all the support and encouragement I could ever want from my fellow followers of Jesus. Why he asked me to become a full-time colleague I shall never know, but his friendship and guidance have certainly been the making of me.

He hasn't done violence to my temperament or character, but I realise I'm still morbidly fascinated by death, a trait I've always put down to my being deprived of my mirror self at the most vulnerable stage of my development. What he has done for me is to change my mindset completely. I mean, it's natural for us to think of life coming first, isn't it, only to be followed by death? That's perfectly understandable, given the standpoint from which we view things. But on no fewer than four separate occasions in barely three years, Jesus led me to see things differently. So much so that I now understand that at the deepest and most meaningful level, the reverse is true. Life – real, undying life – comes after death. Death, in fact, gives birth to life.

Now, just in case you may be thinking that all that sounds close to bordering on mystical nonsense, let me assure you that in the earlier stages of my discipleship I would have reacted in exactly the same way. But Jesus is, among so many other things, a master teacher. He started with us where we were, and took us on so patiently from what we knew to what was new. The first step in his enlargement of our understanding happened wholly unexpectedly.

In the course of one of our tours round Galilee, we were climbing the path into the village of Nain. The first indication we had that a funeral was taking place was the sound of the traditional weeping and wailing, wafted to our ears on the warm morning breeze. Then the sad little procession came into view, slowly wending its way to the village cemetery. Andrew and I were at the front of our group, and Jesus motioned to us to observe the usual courtesies by asking whose death was being mourned. The news that it was a young man who was his widowed mother's only son moved Jesus deeply. He came forward, spoke to the bereaved mother, and asked the pall-bearers to lower the bier to the ground. Then he simply touched the swathed corpse and told the young man to get up. To gasps of amazement all round, the young man did just that, and Jesus gave him back to his mother.

Told like that, the bald facts convey nothing of the impact of the event, which reverberated far beyond the confines of the village and its immediate neighbourhood; but for me, at least, it gained immeasurably in significance when set in the context of two similar acts of Jesus. One took place at Capernaum, where no less a personage than the president of the synagogue there, Jairus by name, came himself to beg Jesus to heal his sick twelve-year-old daughter. But there were so many people blocking the street that before we could get there friends arrived to tell Jairus that his little girl had died.

I heard Jesus say to him, "Don't be afraid – just believe." However, by the time we reached the house, full-scale professional mourning was already under way. I was one of the nine disciples who just could not get inside for the crush of people already there. Later, though, Peter, James, and John told the rest of us everything that had happened.

For me, what was most telling was Jesus's interpretation of that death: "she is not dead, but asleep." Mulling over that afterwards, it seemed pretty obvious to me that what Jesus was saying was that death is not the end and that rising from death is as normal as waking from sleep.

A further stage in Jesus's development of our understanding of death was, if anything, even more dramatic. News came through that Lazarus, a very close friend at Bethany, had died. We were amazed when Jesus proposed that we go there – we'd only just prudently moved out of the area because of the very real threat of a lynching at the hands of the mob. We positively argued with him about it, but when it became obvious that he was determined to go back, I just shrugged my shoulders, turned to the others, and said something to the effect that we might as well go with him and all die together. I did, however, notice that he again made the point, as he had done in the case of Jairus's daughter, that death is not the complete annihilation we perhaps understandably assume that it is.

He said, "Our friend Lazarus has fallen asleep, but I am going there to awaken him." It was only when some of us muttered that he'd stand a better chance of recovery if he was left to sleep in peace that Jesus had to say bluntly, "Lazarus is dead."

Now Jairus's daughter had only just died when Jesus raised her to life again. And the widow of Nain's son had been prepared for burial and was being carried to his grave. But Lazarus was more dead than either of them, if that was possible. By the time we got to Bethany, he'd already been buried for four days. But it seemed as if the greater the challenge, the more it drew out of Jesus, not just in terms of power, but also in terms of his revelation of himself.

In a calm, quiet voice, Jesus said to Lazarus's sister, Martha, "I am the resurrection and the life. Those who believe in me, even though they die, will live." Words like those from anyone else could only have been put down to mental derangement. Jesus astonishingly vindicated them, and himself, by summoning Lazarus back to life there and then, in full view of scores of gawping onlookers.

My mind, my nerves, and my emotions were all reeling from the totally unforeseeable impact of these unimaginable experiences, but I was sure that my understanding of Jesus, and of the light his words and deeds let in on the mystery of life and the problem of death, had expanded immeasurably. Yet how little I had really absorbed was cruelly brought home to me when Jesus himself died. We were all devastated by the apparently total collapse of all we had given ourselves to so completely for the three best years of our lives. My precarious grasp of what Jesus had so painstakingly taught me, especially about life and death, seemed to disappear without trace. When the remaining ten disciples told me that they had seen Jesus alive barely twenty-four hours after he had been buried, all my sturdy native common sense came to the surface. I assumed that they had all fallen victim to some kind of group hallucination that made them think that they had actually seen what they desperately wanted to see. I stoutly declared my determination not to be taken in by any such mass self-deception.

No one will ever be able to enter fully into the experience I had a week later. All eleven of us were together, still cowering behind locked doors in case we were marked down as the authorities' next target. In a break in our conversation, I had the uncanny experience of being absolutely certain that I heard Jesus's voice. I spun round – he was standing there, hands outstretched, with the most understanding expression I have ever seen on anyone's face.

"See my hands," he said. The wounds made by six-inch spikes hammered through his wrists were still red and angry. He took off his clothes. "Look at my side," he said. "Doubt no longer, but believe."

There was a lump in my throat, and my eyes were swimming with tears. Dizzy with relief, I fell to my knees, and sobbed, "My Lord and my God!"

With that gentleness which accommodates the differing needs of every single individual temperament, he accepted that my belief needed to be based on the evidence of my physical senses, but he also remarked, "Blessed are those who have not seen, and yet have come to belief."

As we talked over all this later, Philip reminded me that on the night he was betrayed, Jesus had said that anyone who saw him, saw the Father also. I remembered that that was the occasion when, in response to his comment that we knew the way to the place where he was going, I had said, "Lord, we do not know where you are going. How can we know the way?" Now that his conquest of death has had time to prove itself an indisputable fact, I can understand far more deeply his response to me then. He himself is the way for us through life and through death. He himself is the truth, about man and about God. The whole point and purpose of his own life and death and life restored, is that we too may have life – his life – and have it in all its fullness.

PAUL

From Paul, Apostle of Christ Jesus by the will and command of God,
To Gamaliel, Revered teacher in the things of God:

Grace, mercy, and peace from God our Father and the Lord Jesus Christ.

I have had it in mind for a long time to write to you, Sir, in order to
acquaint you with what has befallen me since my student days with
you in Jerusalem. How long ago those days seem now – and how much
has happened since then! Our paths have not crossed since that early
follower of the new Way, Stephen, was tried by the Sanhedrin and
executed on a charge of blasphemy – do you still remember it? I shall
never be able to forget the look of utter joy and pure ecstasy on that
young man's face as he stood totally alone, claiming that he saw heaven
open, and the son of man standing at the right hand of God. I was so
beside myself with righteous rage that I never thought to look for you
and ask you your opinion on the verdict. Indeed, I more or less led the
stampede that hustled him out into the street and through the city gate
to the nearest open space. I remember regarding it as an honour to be
entrusted with the clothes of the men who stripped off in order to be
able to hurl stones at him more energetically.

I realise, of course, that you already know this, and I am sure that
you must long ago have heard, from all sorts of people, that I have for
many years now been a follower of the Way which Stephen professed
and for which he so willingly laid down his life. What I want to do now
is to try to explain to you why I took this step, which I am sure must
have greatly surprised you when you first heard of it. I hope so much
that you did not feel betrayed or slighted by my action, but if you did, I
trust and pray that by the time you reach the end of this letter you will
at least understand, and perhaps be able to accept, what I have done.

To help you towards this, I have to go right back to Stephen's last
moments. From my vantage point at the front of the crowd, I heard him
call out, "Lord Jesus, receive my spirit!" He made no attempt to escape
the stones raining down upon him, but as he collapsed to his knees,
he shouted out the very last thing I would ever have expected to hear

from a man in his extremity: "Lord, do not hold this sin against them!" Try as I might, I simply could not erase that scene, and especially those words, from my mind. In an attempt to shake myself free of them, I threw myself into a positive frenzy of persecution of the followers of this new Way. But all to no avail. I found that the inner peace and strength and joy which had so unnerved me about young Stephen was not confined only to him; it seemed to be a common characteristic, in varying degrees, of all of the (as I thought) poor deluded people whom I arrested and threw into prison.

Absolutely convinced that what I was doing was wholly consonant with the teaching of the Law and the prophets, and therefore honouring to God Himself, I redoubled my efforts. Word reached Jerusalem that the very success of my campaign there had resulted in an outbreak of the heresy in Damascus – presumably as a result of fugitives from justice fleeing there and making gullible converts to their shocking perversion of the faith of the fathers. I was now becoming increasingly desperate to silence the nagging doubts which were beginning to gnaw away at the very heart of my own convictions. I hoped that by stamping out the infection before it could spread any further, I would regain the certainty which I had never lost before but which now seemed to be ebbing away from me ever more rapidly.

Sir, the man you knew as Saul of Tarsus – an Israelite by race of the tribe of Benjamin, a Hebrew of the Hebrews, circumcised on his eighth day, as to the Law, a Pharisee – never reached Damascus. I drove myself and my men relentlessly northward, savagely refusing to allow a break in our journey, even during the hottest part of the day, but my thoughts and doubts and miseries only accelerated into a whirling vortex which bade fair to threaten my very stability and sanity. I remember I was actually at the point of screaming out loud in my anguish when I was stopped dead in my tracks, so suddenly, that I fell to the ground. Even though my eyes were closed, I became aware of a glow altogether different from the brightness of the blazing midday sun. The glow steadily intensified, and as it did so, I realised that all the torment I had increasingly suffered since my brief brush with Stephen had suddenly and completely lifted. In the marvellous light and peace which now flooded my whole being, I heard a quiet voice insistently asking, "Saul, Saul, why do you persecute me?"

I stammered, "Who are you, Lord?" but I knew I did not need to ask; indeed, I had answered my own question.

But my escort of soldiers told me afterwards that they heard the answer as clearly as I did: "I am Jesus, whom you are persecuting." So the man who entered Damascus at the end of that journey was the man who has since realised that he has become a new creation in Christ – so much so, that he has taken a new name, to signify that he has begun a new life.

But I am so anxious that you should understand that I have not disowned the faith you so convincingly expounded to me – indeed, the reverse is true. You taught me that all the long centuries of our history were a preparation for the coming of God's Chosen One, the Messiah. Noone could have had a better teacher than I had in you; noone could have laid a firmer foundation, for faith and for life, than you did for me. But I am not writing in the first flush of a new convert's enthusiasm. You of all people will appreciate that a wholly life-changing experience of the kind that I have been through needs time and thought and prayer for it to be understood and assimilated.

I, therefore, went first to Arabia before returning to Damascus and later spent six or seven years back at home in Tarsus. In that time, I put to full use all that you had taught me about the Scriptures and the right interpretation of them. As a result, it has been steadily borne in on me, at the deepest levels of my understanding, that all the promises of God, and all the hopes and longings of our people, have been met in Jesus of Nazareth. For God raised him from death – and of that I am an unshakeable witness, since I myself have heard him no less surely than I once heard you, and I have seen him just as clearly as I used to see you. The new age you so fervently looked for has, in our own lifetime, broken in on this present evil age; by raising the crucified Jesus from death, God has proclaimed him as Messiah.

God's intervention to save his people, so long-awaited through all the bygone ages, has now actually occurred.

But there is more to it than that. That underlying, ongoing tension in the Scriptures that you and I used to wrestle with together, between God's salvation for His chosen people Israel only and the apparently contradictory insistence that all nations would nevertheless share in that blessing, has been resolved. The altogether new thing about the Christian Way is that God was in Christ, reconciling the world to himself. The eternal truth that "The Lord our God is one Lord" means that he is God for all the world, not just one part of it, and in breaking down the greatest barrier of all, that between himself and the human race, he has demolished all the lesser barriers which followed on from that one – the barriers between masters and servants, between old and young, between men and women – and yes, even the barrier between Jews and Gentiles.

So the startling message of the new Christian Way is that we are now potentially all one in Christ Jesus – there are no distinctions of any kind. As sin and death previously enslaved everyone, regardless of race or religion, sex or status, so now the defeat of sin at the cross of Christ, and of death by his resurrection, means that everyone, not merely a select few only, can now enter into the freedom and life which Jesus has made available to us. The true Israel, the new Israel, now comprises all believing men and women, of every race and age – for belief, accepting what God has done for us, can alone bring us to salvation. We can never earn it – no one has ever kept the whole of the Law, nor ever could. The good news is that in his immeasurable grace, his undeserved kindness, God in Christ has himself made full provision for the meeting of the entire needs of the whole human race.

I cannot close, dear Gamaliel, without trying to explain to you the reason for the confidence I have in the message I now proclaim. Will you understand if I confide in you that as well as seeing and hearing Jesus physically here on earth after he was raised to life, I have also communed with him spiritually in heaven? No words can ever begin to convey the inexpressible rapture I then experienced; but I was granted a glimpse of the full glory of Christ, reigning with all authority over heaven and earth. Meditating on this afterwards, I realised that I had come full circle and was now exactly where Stephen had been all those years before. Perhaps it is for me to follow eventually the martyr's path which Stephen pioneered; if so, so be it. I have learnt, through all the vicissitudes of my Apostleship, to be content. I am only so grateful that I can, with a clear conscience, affirm in the presence of God and of Christ Jesus, who will judge the living and the dead, that I have fought a good fight, that I have finished my race, and that I have kept the faith. And so, farewell. The Lord be with your spirit.

About the Author

David Gurney was born in Sussex and bred in Kent. Educated in the English grammar school system, he took four degrees at the University of London; his PhD is in the history of early modern English education. He is a member of Mensa and a Fellow of the Royal Society of Arts.

As well as writing, he enjoys classical music and holds a post as an organist and director of music.

He has won prizes for words and music of hymns and has produced a CD of his own choral compositions. His *A Good Fight – Paul's Journal* was his first book, published in 2000 by St. Pauls Publishing, London, and some of his poetry has been printed privately.

Just like Us is one of five studies he has produced of characters associated with Bible stories; he has also written a series of short studies for small groups, entitled *Would You Believe It?*' a simple attempt to present Christian theology in terms appropriate to twenty-first-century thought.

About the Book

Just like Us is a vivid snapshot of the possible reactions of no fewer than twenty-one characters who came into contact with Jesus of Nazareth. It ranges over a wide spectrum of individuals, from Elizabeth, the mother of John the Baptist, to Paul, Apostle to the Gentiles.

The studies are clustered around the birth of Jesus, his death, and his resurrection, and they afford a fascinating glimpse of how representatives from every walk of life, from kings to fishermen, could have responded to the unique personality of the most influential person in history.